Let's Make

AMERICA

GOOD Again

Let's Make
AMERICA
GOOD Again

BILL BROWN

LIBERTY HILL PRESS

Liberty Hill Press
2301 Lucien Way #415
Maitland, FL 32751
407.339.4217
www.libertyhillpublishing.com

Unless otherwise indicated, Scripture quotations taken from the
Revised Standard Version (RSV). Copyright © 1946, 1952, and
1971 the Division of Christian Education of the National Council
of the Churches of Christ in the United States of America. Used
by permission. All rights reserved.

Scripture quotations taken from the Holy Bible, New International
Version (NIV). Copyright © 1973, 1978, 1984, 2011 by Biblica,
Inc.™. Used by permission. All rights reserved.

Printed in the United States of America.

Paperback ISBN-13: 978-1-6312-9472-3
Dust Jacket ISBN-13: 978-1-6312-9619-2
eBook ISBN-13:   978-1-6312-9474-7

CONTENTS

PROLOGUE

IT WAS NOVEMBER 1970, and three of us stood beneath the covered portico of a business on the southwest corner across from the Commonwealth Club in San Francisco. As I recall, we had a view of most of the club, which covered almost all of a city block in north San Francisco. On this particular day, the guest speaker at the Commonwealth Club was to be South Vietnamese General, Nguyen Cao Ky, who had served as Prime Minister of Vietnam for a time.

Across the street to the west of the Commonwealth Club was a church with a low brick wall around most of the property. We could see over that wall as hundreds of demonstrators were adding to the stockpile of rocks, bricks, bottles, marbles, steel balls—things that, as it turned out, were to be thrown at police once the demonstration against the Vietnamese War got into full swing.

The part of the block on which the Club was situated that we could see had a cordon of police officers clad in full riot gear, including acrylic-shielded helmets, protective vests, and larger hand-held shields, also of acrylic. You couldn't see their faces, but their stance indicated that they were ready. The officers, each equipped with a long riot stick, were lined up three rows deep and stood at parade rest while the crowd across the street worked itself into the fever that always preceded the taunting, cursing, and challenging directed toward the police. The commander of the San Francisco Riot Squad, who held the rank of captain, stood just behind his men, urging them to stay calm.

The demonstrators now began pouring over the wall, filling the street on the south side of the church. A single officer on a three-wheeled motorbike made an aggressive run down one side of the street, forcing the demonstrators back up onto the sidewalk. When he looked back in the direction he'd come and saw that he was alone, he slowed his vehicle to turn and head back toward where the other officers had formed their line. As he turned, one of the demonstrators yanked the officer's helmet off and another hit him on top of the head with a brick. In an instant, the officer fell to the ground, unconscious and covered in his own blood. The Riot Squad Commander dispatched six to eight officers to disperse the crowd and rescue the fallen officer. These men carried the unconscious policeman back behind their cordon line, and in a matter of a few minutes an ambulance arrived to take the wounded officer to the hospital. The three of us had observed the entire incident, and we all thought the officer had lost so much blood that he might even be dead.

Now that there was blood in the water, literally and figuratively, the demonstrators grew bolder. Some of them flooded into the street east of the churchyard, coming to within ten to fifteen feet of the police line; shouting, cursing and spitting at the officers. The captain commanding the Riot Squad continued to calm his troops with admirable success... until the first brick came sailing over the heads of the lead demonstrators and struck the face mask of an officer in the second row. Stunned, the man dropped to his knees. Another officer from the rank behind moved up to take his place. Now you could feel an electric charge in the air. The game was on. In a moment, a whole barrage of rocks, half-bricks, bottles, and marbles began to rain down upon the officers. Two more fell. Finally, the captain had seen enough. He raised his baton along with his voice:

"Clear those people out of the street and out of that church yard!"

The first two ranks of officers charged across the street, batons at the ready. Demonstrators were scrambling, running over each other trying to get out of the way. The slow ones, and those who mistakenly thought they wanted to fight, paid a price. The San Francisco Riot Squad did what had been asked of them. There was a brief hand-to-hand skirmish, and then all of the demonstrators broke and ran.

I looked up to see a man in a business suit running and stumbling across the street toward us from the church yard. He saw how we were dressed (in business suits) and perhaps assumed that we were FBI agents or police officials. He was holding a handkerchief to his forehead, but it was doing little to stop the flow of blood.

"Did you see what that officer did to me?" he screamed.

"Which officer?" I asked.

He looked around, but of course, he wasn't able to pick out his assailant from among the melee.

"He deliberately hit me with his baton, and I wasn't doing anything!"

"Where were you when you got hit?" I asked.

He turned and pointed toward the church.

"What were you doing there? Didn't you know what was going on in that yard? Did that not seem to be a sort of dangerous place to be?"

"Well, he had no business hitting me. I didn't do anything!"

He was almost crying now.

"They were kind of busy dodging rocks and bottles. Do you think that officer had the time to ask you, 'Pardon me, sir? Did you happen to throw a rock at me?' That officer had been told by his supervisor to run those people out of the church yard—you know, the people that had been throwing stuff at them for several minutes. That officer was doing what he had been told to do."

There was nothing about the incident in the *San Francisco Chronicle*. Not the following day, nor in later editions, and there were many more violent demonstrations against the war in Vietnam over the next couple of years that several of us covered in our capacity as FBI agents in San Francisco. The late '60s and early '70s was truly a bitter era in the Bay region.

Several years later, after the presidency of Ronald Reagan, I had hoped that kind of anti-American sentiment was *passé*—but no. *It had only gone dormant for a while.*

SECTION I

The Constitution and Religion

Chapter 1

WHAT OR WHERE ARE WE AS AMERICANS TODAY?

Morality is essential, and all the incidents of morality, — as, justice to the subject, and personal liberty. Montesquieu says—"Countries are well cultivated, not as they are fertile, but as they are free;" and the remark holds not less, but more, true of the culture of men than of the tillage of land. And the highest proof of civility is, that the whole public action of the State is directed on securing the greatest good of the greatest number.

Ralph Waldo Emerson

And let us with caution indulge the supposition that morality can be maintained without religion. Whatever may be conceded to the influence of refined education on minds of peculiar structure, reason and experience both forbid us to expect that national morality can prevail in exclusion of religious principle.

Washington's Farewell Address, 1796

AN AMERICAN CONSERVATIVE could be forgiven if he were to ask, "*Can our country survive another three or four years of the kind of bitterness, rancor, and incivility that permeates the very atmosphere of our nation's capital?*" And furthermore, "*Can two parties with agendas so diverse and completely incompatible continue to govern?*"

Several years ago, I wrote a blog piece that, if it were applicable then, it's exponentially timelier now. That article, written during the throes of the Obama administration at a time when it seemed impossible that the division between liberals and conservatives could be any deeper, addressed the question of whether America could survive the stark diversity between the aims of the two political parties at that time. Well, we certainly found out with the election of Donald Trump as President that yes, things could definitely get worse. I cannot recall a period in our history where the ideas embraced by the two political parties as to what America is and what it stands for were further apart. And it's difficult to find any room for compromise.

Where do we go from here? Will the socialist/communist ideas of Alexandria Ocasio-Cortez and Bernie Sanders carry the day, or is there yet hope that America will once again be the beacon on a hill, the guiding light for countries the world over as to what a civilized nation can accomplish working together in peaceful cooperation? That latter prospect has never been dimmer.

Which direction will America take in the coming years? Will we succumb to the siren song of socialism—that all citizens (some would include all illegal aliens) are entitled to almost everything—free—gratis—and devolve into a full-blown socialist nation like Venezuela?

Little more than twenty years ago, Venezuela was the fourth-wealthiest country in the world. The production of oil made them rich beyond their dreams. But now? Now they are stuck in grinding poverty and a shortage of practically everything that families need for survival. The inflation rate in April of 2019 was—and this is a tough figure to fathom—289, 973 percent!

Is that where we are headed, or will we pursue the more moderate socialism of Western Europe and settle for a slightly more modest level of poverty (but poverty, nonetheless) for all except the ruling class (there is always a "ruling class," even in socialism) accompanied by high taxes?

Though Las Vegas would rate the odds extremely low, we could yet opt to follow the course that our Founding Fathers laid out for us and continue with a democratic republic as our form of government.

A sizeable proportion of America's population rejects the idea posited by our forefathers that Christianity should be the guide we follow in pursuit of equitable and just government. Although one could see this coming since the 1960s, probably none of us were quite ready for such widespread and absolute rejection of all things Christian. What a dramatic change!

How did we get here, to the point where, from elementary school all the way through college, including our Law schools, secular humanists are in control of our institutions of learning? They have an almost monopolistic lock on all our forms of media—print, television and movies—and one house of Congress.

How could this have happened?

This book is not a diatribe against all the evil in America, and how America is going to hell in a hand-basket. Oh, no. There are still millions of Americans who are as concerned as you are about the problems attending our nation just now: men and women who work every day, trying to properly care for their children and attempting to teach them the difference between right and wrong. There remains a solid cadre of men and women of excellent character who are seeking ways to make certain that this country continues to be the Land of Opportunity; the best place in the world to make a home and rear children. If these efforts are to be successful, what will be the glue that binds our nation's wounds and restores calm to our land?

Chapter 2

FAITH IN THE DEMOCRATIC REPUBLIC

Our Cause is Noble. It is the cause of Mankind
—George Washington

The Founding Fathers and Christianity

READERS WHO ARE secular humanists (and I'm sure there will be a few) will have a difficult time understanding what I would outline for us as the only foundation suitable for a democratic republic, the form of government that America has enjoyed for almost 240 years. I implore you, however, to persevere in this book and genuinely make an effort to consider it. Our Founding Fathers understood well that only a government based upon the Judeo-Christian ethos provided so much freedom to its citizens.

The Founding Fathers considered that man might become less earnest in his concern for the rights of others. They thought it unlikely to present a problem, *as long as* the citizens of America remained true to those Christian convictions that guided their everyday activities. Why would a nation and a people be so foolish as to reject the leadership of a loving God? If you doubt that the Founding Fathers had any such considerations in mind when they drafted and approved the Constitution, let us review what some of these men wrote and said about Christianity and the Constitution, contemporaneous with the adoption of that document. These men were thoroughly convinced that America was, and would forever remain, a Christian nation. They knew that the success of this experiment with democracy depended heavily upon the citizenry being able to practice the kind of love and respect for the rights of others, along with the kind of discipline that would see that the rights of all were assured.

John Adams, our second president:

> "Our Constitution was made only for a moral and religious people. It is wholly inadequate to the government of any other."
> – in a speech made to the Massachusetts Militia (October 11, 1798)

> "Human passions unbridled by morality and religion ... would break the strongest cords of our Constitution as a whale goes through a net."
> – from the John Adams Historical Society

> "The general principles upon which the Fathers achieved independence were the general principles of Christianity ... I will avow that I believed and now believe that those general principles of Christianity are as eternal and immutable as the existence and attributes of God."
> – Excerpts from a letter to Thomas Jefferson

> On April 18, 1775, a British soldier ordered him (John Adams), John Hancock, and others to "disperse in the name of George, the Sovereign King of England." Adams responded to him: *"We*

recognize no sovereign but God, and no king but Jesus!"
— faithofourfathers.net

Thomas Jefferson:

"Among the most inestimable of our blessings, also is... that of liberty to worship our Creator in the way we think most agreeable to His will; a liberty deemed in other countries incompatible with good government and yet proved by our experiment to be its best support." (This describes freedom *of* religion, not freedom *from* religion.)- From a letter dated November 18, 1807–The University of Virginia Press

"The doctrines of Jesus are simple and tend to the happiness of man."
-*Jefferson's Religion,* by Stephen J. Vicchio

"Of all the systems of morality, ancient or modern which have come under my observation, none appears to me so pure as that of Jesus."
Thomas Jefferson
Letter to W. Canby, 1813 Jefferson's religion by NC Howland, Lulu Press, 2014

"God who gave us life gave us liberty. And can the liberties of a nation be thought secure when we have removed their only firm basis, a conviction in the minds of the people that these liberties are a gift from God? That they are not to be violated but with His wrath? Indeed I tremble for my country when I reflect that God is just, and that His justice cannot sleep forever."–Source: Merrill . D. Peterson, ed., Jefferson Writings, (New York: Literary Classics of the United States, Inc., 1984), Vol. IV, p. 289.

"The constitutional freedom of religion [is] the most inalienable and sacred of all human rights." -Thomas Jefferson: Virginia Board of Visitors Minutes, 1819.

Benjamin Franklin:

"The longer I live, the more convincing proofs I see of this truth—that God governs in the affairs of men. I also believe that without His concurring aid, we shall succeed in this political building [the drafting of the Constitution] no better than the builders of Babel [the Biblical tower to heaven that collapsed]." (He was in his eighties at the time he said this.)
- Benjamin Franklin
Constitutional Convention Address on Prayer delivered Thursday, June 28, 1787, Philadelphia, PA

George Washington:

"Let us with caution indulge the supposition that morality can be maintained without religion. Reason and experience both forbid us to expect that national morality can prevail in exclusion of religious principles."

– from General George Washington's Farewell Address to his Army.

"What students would learn in American schools above all is the religion of Jesus Christ."
– George Washington, from a speech to the Delaware Indian Chiefs given on May 12, 1779.

"To the distinguished character of patriot, it should be our highest glory to add the more distinguished character of Christian."
- from a speech General Washington gave on May 2, 1778 at Valley Forge. (Still wonder whether Washington was a Christian?)

James Madison:

"We've staked our (the American nation's) future on our ability to follow the Ten Commandments with all our heart."
– James Madison–From The Cell by Chris Hambleton, Xulon Press, page 30, 2010

Patrick Henry ("Give me liberty or give me death!"):

"The Bible is worth all the other books which have ever been printed." -Gatsbe Exchange Famous Authors and Quotes

John Jay, writer of five of the eighty-five Federalist Papers and the first Chief Justice of the United States Supreme Court:

"Providence has given to our people the choice of
their rulers and it is the duty as well as the privilege
and interest of our Christian Nation to select and
prefer Christians for their rulers."
—Founding Fathers Quote #675

Charles Carroll, Maryland delegate and signer of the Declaration
of Independence:

"Without morals a republic cannot subsist any
length of time; they therefore who are decrying
the Christian religion, whose morality is so sub-
lime and pure... are undermining the foundation
of morals, the best security for the duration of free
government."
- The-american-catholic.com

Go back and read that statement a second time. It cannot be
better said. Those words are as applicable today as they were then.
That is the clearest statement of why we, the citizens of the United
States, must not allow the faith upon which our nation was founded
to be relegated to the ash bin of history by this country's so-called
"intelligentsia."

Is it possible that all thirty-nine of the delegates to that convention who signed the American Constitution were somehow
mentally impaired? Within the lower quadrant of the IQ scale?
Illiterate? Did Europe empty its prisons and insane asylums in the
16th and 17th centuries and send defective people here to America,
as Fidel Castro of Cuba did in the late 1970s? Was everyone who
participated in the drafting of the Constitution appointed *because*
he was among the most mentally challenged men of his colony?

If you think so, it would do little good to suggest that you read something about the lives and contributions of the Founding Fathers.

This is certainly not a denigration of the relative intelligence of Alexandria Ocasio-Cortez, but do you really believe she is as widely read, as well-educated and as intelligent as, say, Alexander Hamilton? Of course, we have no accurate means of measuring such things now, but I feel safe in saying Hamilton would have been eligible for the Mensa Society.

Hamilton was only the most intelligent, in this writer's opinion, in a room full of intellectual giants—Thomas Jefferson, James Madison, Benjamin Franklin, to name a few. While Jefferson was not a part of the Constitutional Convention, much of the language in the U S Constitution came from the Constitution Jefferson had a major part in drafting for the Commonwealth of Virginia.

No, it was not a lack of intellect that persuaded our Founders to recommend so strongly that America stay the course of Christianity and Christian leadership for the fledgling nation. As the signers of the Declaration of Independence vowed… "And for the support of this Declaration, with a firm reliance on the protection of Divine Providence, we mutually pledge to each other our Lives, our Fortunes, and our sacred Honor." That sounds like the affirmation of some very patriotic, dedicated men consecrating themselves for God and country.

Our legal system was fashioned after the British common law, thought then to be the most considerate of the rights of ordinary citizens. It was a good system. Not perfect, but good. The founders believed that America should adopt British common law but undergird it with the principles of the Christian religion, and that these would be the only realistic bases for a democratic republic—one that would offer freedoms and liberties never before seen in any governing system. Unless the citizens of this government were motivated by something more than their own self-interests and greed, this experiment with a democratic republic would be an abject failure, for surely only a people striving to do what was right and in the best interests of all citizens could survive in such a free society. That concern for the rights and welfare of other citizens was completely compatible with the Christian religion, which is the only religion except Judaism I know of that teaches its practitioners, as Jesus is recorded as saying in the book of Matthew in the New Testament, "You shall love the Lord your God with all your heart and with all your soul and with all your mind. This is the great and first commandment. And a second is like it: You shall love your neighbor as yourself" (Matt. 22:37-39–RSV) (Also found in the 6th Chapter of Deuteronomy).

Not tolerance. Not acceptance, but love—even of those who, as Jesus said in Matthew 5, "spitefully use you."

Indeed, Alexander Hamilton and many others predicted that, because of all the freedoms provided in the Constitution, it would not be long before even Christians would begin to take advantage of these liberties at the expense of other citizens.

When you think about it, Christians are, or should be, easy marks for those not encumbered with a conscience or concern for the rights of others. Christians are generally much more trusting of people than non-Christians are because they tend to associate more commonly with other Christians, who they consider trustworthy. They tend to not question the motives of other Christians or wonder whether they are trying to cheat them. Furthermore, Christians are less inclined to sue those who have taken advantage of them or report such incidents to the authorities. Now, they will be more careful in future dealings with individuals who have cheated them in the past and might tighten up their business practices in general, but they will likely continue to trust others; that is the way Christians generally choose to live.

They will also tend to feel that an individual who cheated them in a business deal or lied about them to get them into trouble will be harmed more in the long run than they, the alleged victims, will. Even if that were not so, all things, whether good or evil, will be sorted out in God's kingdom. Besides, Romans 8:28 says, "And we know that in all things God works for the good of those who love him, who have been called according to his purpose". (NIV of the Bible). God will make it right.

Chapter 3

WHAT DOES CHRISTIANITY HAVE TO DO WITH GOVERNMENT?

THE FIRST AMENDMENT to the Constitution says, "Congress shall make no law respecting an establishment of religion, or prohibiting the free exercise thereof..."

This amendment has been misinterpreted over the years. Our Founding Fathers never meant to separate state and church, but instead just wanted to make sure that the government does not interfere with religion. Especially that it does not officially establish one particular religion or denomination over another or establish non-religion over religion. The secular humanists in America are trying to establish non-religion over religion.

Many on the left would say that the church should have absolutely *nothing* to do with government, that the Founding Fathers intended that there should be a "high wall of separation" between church and state.

That is a lie.

It is a strongly-held premise, particularly by American secularists, that there should be a *high wall of separation between Church and State*. Whether that premise is based upon a misunderstanding or upon a lie—deliberately misconstruing the statements of James Madison and Thomas Jefferson regarding the relationship between church (small *c*) and the government, state or federal, has yet to be determined.

But what does 'separation of church and state' mean? Was that idea a prevalent thought in the minds of the framers of the Constitution—that the church, in terms of the members of various denominations, should be forbidden to participate in political matters? To have acted upon such ideas would have disenfranchised most of the population of that era. Since, as we shall demonstrate later, a majority of members of the committee to draft a new constitution were believing, practicing Christians, such a view would have excluded most members of that august body from being able to vote on the very document they were crafting.

All secularists cite the words of our third president of the United States, Thomas Jefferson, to show that he believed that the church had no role in government. Those words to which they refer were contained in a letter by which Jefferson responded to a plea from a group of baptists in Danbury, Connecticut. This group elicited Jefferson's aid in securing for them the privilege of running for and holding office in that state—both things they had heretofore been denied because of their church affiliation as baptists.

Let's have a closer look at that.

From 1639, when Connecticut was an independent colony, they were persuaded to adopt the Fundamental Orders, which were operative until 1818, when Connecticut's first state constitution was ratified. Prior to 1818, "...almost every aspect of life in Connecticut was controlled by the 'Standing Order', by which had been established an elite group of intellectuals, politicians and religious leaders," according to George Curley in his 2007 master's thesis, *The Fall of the Standing Order: Connecticut 1800-1818*.

Congregationalism was the established religion, and politicians were uniformly members of the Congregational Church. In addition, Yale College, established and overseen by the Congregational

Church, produced the intellectuals and ministers whose leadership provided justification for the continuance of traditional Connecticut politics.

Timothy Dwight, a minister in the Congregationalist Church and the 8th President of Yale College, was perhaps the staunchest defender of the Standing Order and "steady habits," as he called it, in politics. He loved the "stability" that the Standing Order provided the colony and saw no problem with excluding non-Congregationalists and others not associated with Yale College, from holding elective office in Connecticut.

The absence of a voice in selecting those who led them was, however, only part of the problem for the baptists of Connecticut. And the Baptist church wasn't alone. Other churches and many other citizens of Connecticut were also forced to endure the 'Standing Order.' Because Congregationalism was the official religion in Connecticut, all citizens of that state were forced to pay a tithe of ten percent of their income to the Congregationalist Church. Oh, there was a high-sounding defense for that seemingly unfair practice—the support of religious education, with the obvious inference that no other church apart from the Congregationalists would or could provide such instruction.

Some early Connecticut Republicans, influenced by what they had learned about the initial democratic aspect of the French Revolution, and by positions espoused by Thomas Jefferson (a fierce Francophile), began to agitate for equal rights. Among their membership were former Federalists and Congregationalists, but there were also Episcopalians, Baptists, and later, Unitarians and Universalists who were angered at the Congregationalists' refusal to allow them equal status. All of these denominations were more liberal and tolerant than members of the Standing Order.

The Republicans espoused a broadening of the electoral franchise, the severing of the tax-supported link between the state and the Congregational church, and ultimately, the drafting and ratification of a new state constitution to replace the Royal Charter of 1662.

In other words, the new Connecticut State Constitution, when it was finally adopted in 1817, gave, for the first time, Baptists, Unitarians, Puritans—practitioners of all religions and those who practiced no religion at all—an equal political footing with members of the Congregational Church.

Remember, it was a *state* (or colony) that forced its citizens to contribute to a Church (capital *C*) chosen by the *state*.

A movement sprang up in the colonies called 'disestablishment' (referring to the disestablishment of *any particular church* as the official church of a state or colony) which, in essence, created a fight over religious taxes, and eliminating taxes was the crucial act of disestablishment in many states, not just Connecticut. In Virginia, a proposal to use tax revenues to support Christian teachers was so unpopular that, after its defeat, the victors were able to pass Thomas Jefferson's Bill for Establishing Religious Freedom, which included the provision that "no man shall be compelled to frequent or support any religious worship, place or ministry whatsoever."

As early as 1783, Connecticut's legislature had begun passing laws exempting certain people from religious taxation in an effort to retain at least a portion of the Congregationalists' ecclesiastical hegemony within that state. After financial support for state churches (Congregationalists) declined, however, the legislature tightened the exemption requirements in 1790. These renewed religious requirements—the combination of paying taxes or having to show church membership and attendance—once again fueled opposition. A year later, in 1791, the strict requirements were repealed, effectively disestablishing the state church in Connecticut.

In Virginia, citizens could worship at any church they chose. Regardless of where they worshipped, however, they had to pay a tithe of 10 percent to the Anglican Church (Church of England).

From the time the first British immigrants settled in the Commonwealth of Virginia in 1607, the British crown had granted the Anglican Church special privileges by declaring it the established church of the commonwealth. Religious hegemony and social dominance went hand-in-hand. Virginia was governed by large tobacco planters who were closely associated with the Anglican Church. In *Wellspring of Liberty*, the historian John Ragosta writes, "To any eighteenth-century Virginian, the legal and social dominance of the Church of England was unmistakable."

(Doesn't that sound similar to the situation in Connecticut)?

In Virginia, attempts by other churches to establish equality with the Anglicans were not just ignored, but in some cases was punished—by the Anglican Church and by sympathetic local sheriffs. Baptists recruited new audiences among the poor who found the baptists' emphasis on the equality of all believers appealing. Dissenting ministers (mainly Baptist) who, for the most part, held their services outdoors so that there would be room for all comers, at least symbolically returned to the simplicity of earlier days. There was no room in these settings for the prestige of gentry grandeur and the front pew status found within the official religion.

Gaining influence with the citizenry of the state did not come without a cost. The colonial Anglican gentry responded to the presence of preachers from other denominations with force. They broke up meetings and open-air sermons, imprisoned "heretic" preachers, and incited mobs to whip, burn, and stone repeat offenders. Some historians posit that Virginian dissenters arguably suffered the worst religious persecution in antebellum America.

In the 1770s, prompted by the dissenters, the campaign to secure full religious liberty in Virginia led to a flurry of public petitions, which in turn threatened to undermine the commonwealth's cohesion at the same time that political sentiment against Great Britain hinted of a coming war for independence. The leaders of the commonwealth faced a dilemma: whether to make concessions to the nonconformist sects, or fail to do so, and risk splitting their military support base at the very point that the growing revolutionary movement most required that assistance.

Dissenters used the fact that the colony of Virginia needed their active participation as soldiers in the event of a war for independence from Great Britain by promising to join the revolutionary battle *only* if their religious freedom was guaranteed. That pressure finally led to the first major concession. In 1776, the Virginia Convention adopted a Bill of Rights that included a provision for the "free exercise of religion," and stated the claim to that freedom in influential language crafted by George Mason and James Madison:

> That religion, or the duty which we owe to our Creator and the manner of discharging it, can be directed by reason and conviction, not by force or violence; and therefore, all men are equally entitled to the free exercise of religion, according to the dictates of conscience; and that it is the mutual duty of all to practice Christian forbearance, love, and charity towards each other.

I would ask you to notice Christian forbearance—not Islamic, Buddhist, Hindu or secular humanist forbearance. *Christian* forbearance!

That was not enough for the dissenters. They demanded an end to state-enforced tithes and insisted that restrictions on their worship services and marriage ceremonies be removed. (Weddings performed in baptist churches, for instance, were not recognized as legal in Virginia.)

In the face of mounting discontent with the *status quo,* Revolutionary leader Patrick Henry and other privileged members of the planter class continued to support an established church. Henry, while agreeing to a limited form of pluralism, insisted that the state government would still enforce a "general assessment" or tax, for the support of "selected" Christian churches. His proposal would permit individuals to earmark their taxes for the church of their choice, but each taxpayer would be compelled to support one of the officially sanctioned churches.

In the essay, "Memorial and Remonstrance against Religious Assessments," James Madison eloquently laid out reasons why the state had no business supporting Christian instruction, which was the reasoning behind mandated church tithes. Some would have you believe that in this statement, Madison was coming out four-square *against* Christian education. To hold that view requires one to ignore what Madison is alleged to have said after the Constitution was adopted:

> We have staked the whole future of American civilization not upon the power of government, far from it. We have staked the future of all our political institutions upon the capacity of mankind for self-government, upon the capacity of each and all of us to govern ourselves, to control ourselves, to sustain ourselves according to the Ten Commandments.

Did Madison ever say this? We do not have positive information that he did say it. So, we are left to ask, are we only to rely on what non-contemporaries of Madison have reported, or should we simply accept that, since we cannot find those words in extant writing, that they are demonstrably untrue? You decide.

At any rate, the assessment against which Madison argued was not only the assessment of a tithe from non-members to be paid into the coffers of the Anglican Church, but the forced assessment of a tithe to *any* church.

Madison was in agreement with Jefferson that, "citizens should not be judged by their religious beliefs."

That was only tangential to what the struggle against the colonial rulers was all about. While many non-Christians may not see it as a big deal, tithers will understand how the people felt put-upon to be forced to tithe 10 percent of their income to support a church where they were not members, and then have an additional moral or spiritual responsibility to give another 10 percent to the church where they *were* members. That was 20 percent of their income, half of which was taken by a church with many tenets and beliefs they did not subscribe to, and in some instances, adamantly opposed.

The impact of the struggle of Virginia and Connecticut's Protestant Dissenters was far-reaching and spread beyond the borders of their own colonies. By the time the new national Constitution was drafted in 1787, Virginia—a former "bastion of established Anglicanism"—had become the most progressive of the thirteen original states in protecting religious liberties.

What Virginia settlers opposed so strenuously was *being forced to recognize and support the tenets of one church over those of any other.* It was as though the authority of the Anglican Church leader in Virginia was synonymous with the early pope of the Roman Catholic Church who did not accept the legitimacy of any other church. *That* is wrong, as the Roman Catholic Pope erred, in the eyes of Protestants, in calling himself the one and only Vicar of Christ in the early centuries of the church.

Contained in the paragraphs above are some of the passages that progressives utilize to provide "proof positive" for the point that Thomas Jefferson and James Madison, among others, were determined to keep the church from having any influence at all upon the government—what they describe as a "wall of separation between church and state."

In fact, what the colonists of Virginia sought was freedom from paying the assessed tithe that the Colony of Virginia, by and for the Anglican Church, imposed upon most non-Anglican settlers. They reasonably thought it was an unnecessary burden upon them to have to support the Church of England while contributing to the support of the pastor of their own church—be it baptist, Calvinist or whatever. They rejected the idea of having to accept either the religious dogma of the Anglican Church or the part they were expected to play in providing financial supporting to the state church.

The Danbury Baptists of Connecticut sought to 1) end their disbarment from participation in the selection of elected officials, and 2) end the tithe initially required of each of them, to be directed into the coffers of the Congregationalist Church.

To read the above paragraphs about Virginia's and Connecticut's struggle with the official state church (Anglican in Virginia, Congregationalist in Connecticut) as a direct rejection of any involvement of the church (small c) at all in affairs of the state demands willful self-deception. Comments of the Founders at the culmination of their efforts to craft a Constitution provided wise suggestions for practices to ensure that guiding instrument's perpetuation.

You cannot say out of one side of your mouth that a democratic republic, established on any other foundation than the Christian religion, cannot stand, while out of the other side of your mouth you say that you don't want the church or its members to be involved in politics in any way. That makes absolutely no sense. And yet, our progressive opponents would have you believe just that.

Some of you may be old enough to remember when John F. Kennedy became the first Catholic to be elected President of the United States. He felt it necessary to promise the people of America that he would not follow the direction of the Holy Roman Catholic

Church in any decision he might be required to make, but would follow the course of action that would most benefit the citizens of this great country. Many of us assumed that was an answer in search of a question. Who doubted that he would be that kind of president?

Something that all of us need to keep in mind is this: *the Constitution was not written to protect the government from the people, but to protect the people from an overreaching government.* However, in their zeal to reserve for the states all powers not specifically within the purview of the federal government, the framers of the Constitution allowed the respective states to deal with the problem of a state-sponsored church. It should be noted that, while it took a few years, the states *did* wind up doing the right thing.

Neither the states nor the federal government need fear the church (small c) controlling the government—unless the number of practitioners of Islam reaches the level of majority in America, as it has in Iran, Saudi Arabia, Syria, et al. Then, all bets are off.

Bottom line: The Danbury Baptists *did not* ask President Jefferson's assistance in dealing with the Congregationalist Church. No, the church was not the problem. The problem was that the government of the Colony of Connecticut was *forcing* them—yes, *forcing them*—to participate in the *state's* church of preference by means of support via *taxes and mandatory church attendance.* Again, the people of America need to be protected from the overreach of government *at all levels*, and those who do not see the difference between freedom from forced participation in a *state-sponsored religion* (read ISLAM in countries where that religion is near the majority) *and freedom from any mention, in public, of Christianity or its Christ* are willfully blind.

Isn't it amazing that among the people most adamantly against the Christian faith are certain members of our government? It's true. One could easily make the case that the progressive Democrat Party is almost fully under the control of the secular humanists, and no single group has more to lose from the advancement of Christianity than secular humanists—unless it could be the socialists—another appellation that describes a great number of Democrats.

But, progressives do not criticize Islam. In fact, the opposite is true. They will vigorously defend that faith and ensure that *no one* can make an unchallenged denunciation of that belief system. We should be reminded that the communists never criticized Islam, either—or any other religion aside from Christianity.

Why?

Because no other religion is so diametrically opposed to the kind of tenets and strictures that make up communism; none is more incompatible with communism than Christianity.

It is not totally out of the realm of possibility that the reason progressives fight so hard to keep Christianity out of our schools, out of our government, and out of the public marketplace lies in their devotion to these two principal beliefs—secular humanism and socialism/communism.

Strange that progressives/secular humanists/socialists should evince fear lest Christianity obtain a religious hegemony in America and dictate to all liberals what they can and cannot do. The most prominent example one might cite of a religion wresting control of an established government and making such dramatic, life-changing differences was the overthrow of the Shah of Iran in 1979—with invaluable assistance from the American President, Jimmy Carter. Iran had become an ally of the United States, had purchased many tanks and planes from our country, and its military was being trained in the effective use of that equipment by US military personnel—in Iran. The Iranians had become the most westernized of US allies, and the Shah had made great strides in women's rights, among other social and governmental improvements. But, his reforms apparently were not moving fast enough for President Carter and his State

Department, so a coalition of Marxists, Islamic religionists, and other dissenters forced the aging and terminally-ill Shah to abdicate his throne, which he did in the absence of any sign of support from President Carter or the U.S. State Department.

The Ayatollah Khomeini, who had been in exile in Paris, France flew back to Tehran and took control of the Iranian government.

Overnight, Iran changed from a secular government to one in which all shots were called by the Ayatollah—the religious leader of Iranian Islam. American military personnel and petroleum workers had to make a hasty evacuation from Iran, most sending their families out ahead of them, staying behind in order to salvage what they had brought to Iran from America. They had to abandon most of their personal property, anyway. The Iranian military officers were sympathetic to the plight of the Americans, but could do nothing to save them from the wrath of the Ayatollah. Some Americans who did not make it out of Iran were jailed; some were murdered.

Multi-millionaire Ross Perot, who Republicans loved to hate, hired a retired Army Green Beret Lt. Colonel named Bo Gritz to lead a team that flew to Tehran in Perot's private jet. With Perot on board that plane awaiting the outcome, Gritz' team hurriedly made their way to the nearby prison and forcibly removed two Americans, employees of Perot, put them aboard the plane and flew them safely back to America.

Are the progressives/secular humanists/socialists genuinely afraid that Christians might stage such an attempted overthrow of the American government as that which returned the Ayatollah Khomeini to power in Iran?

Tell me you are, and I'll tell you to your face that you are a liar.

Progressives/secular humanists/socialists have nothing to fear from a Christian armed coup. No, those leftist groups only fear *the influence* of Christianity against hegemonic governments; not it's threat to a democratic republic.

Chapter 4

IF NOT CHRISTIANITY, WHAT?

PRESIDENT BARACK OBAMA spoke fondly of the Islam religion, remarking how beautiful was the call to prayer, the Adhan, recited by the mu'azzin in the early morning. He often spoke of the contributions to American culture made by the people of Islam.

Would Islam be an appropriate belief system upon which to build a democratic Republic?

Islam

The BBC summarizes the Five Pillars of Islam as such:

> The Five Pillars of Islam are the five obligations that every Muslim must satisfy in order to live a good and responsible life according to Islam.
>
> The Five Pillars consist of:
>
> - Shahadah: sincerely reciting the Muslim profession of faith
> - Salat: performing ritual prayers in the proper way five times each day
> - Zakat: paying an alms (or charity) tax to benefit the poor and the needy

- Sawm: fasting during the month of Ramadan
- Hajj: pilgrimage to Mecca

Of Islam's concept of God, Religion Resources Online says the following:

> Islam's fundamental theological concept is *tawhīd* — belief in only one god. The Arabic term for God is *Allāh*; most scholars believe it was derived from a combination of the words *al-* (the) and *'ilah* (deity, masculine form), meaning «the god» (*al-ilāh*), but others trace its origin to the Aramaic word *Alāhā*. The first of the Five Pillars of Islam, *tawhīd* is expressed in the *shahadah* (testification), declaring that there is no god but God (Allah), and that Muhammad is God's messenger. In traditional Islamic theology, God is beyond any comprehension; Muslims are not expected to visualize God but to worship and adore him as a protector. Although Muslims believe that Jesus was a prophet, they reject the Christian doctrine of a Trinity, comparing it to polytheism. In Islamic theology, Jesus was just a man, not the son of God; God is described in a chapter (*sura*) of the Qur'an as "...God, the One and Only; God, the Eternal, Absolute; He begetteth not, nor is He begotten; and there is none like unto Him."

There is nothing in those five pillars to indicate an aversion to good order. Perhaps there is an explanation of the verses in the Quran that seem to call for the murder of infidels—those not of the Islam belief. However, there is something either in the Quran itself or in the way that it is being taught and considered by many of its practitioners that enables them to commit all sorts of carnage in the name of Allah. If these murderers are really outside the mainstream of Islam, why are not more leaders of Islam speaking out against them and attempting to control the carnage? Do you honestly believe the Southern Baptists would approve of a marauding band of deacons committing robberies and murders in the name of God?

I feel obliged to include at this point an observation concerning the religion of Islam by a former Prime Minister of Great Britain. Winston Churchill wrote the following in a book called *The River War*, an account of the retaking of the African Sudan from militant Islamists. It was published in 1899 in the United Kingdom by Longmans, Green and Company. Why are the lands occupied by the Palestinians so poor and unproductive in every way? Perhaps the answer lies in the first paragraph below:

> "How dreadful are the curses which Mohammedanism lays on its votaries! Besides the fanatical frenzy, which is as dangerous in a man as hydrophobia in a dog, there is this fearful fatalistic apathy. The effects are apparent in many countries. Improvident habits, slovenly systems of agriculture, sluggish methods of commerce, and insecurity of property exist wherever the followers of the Prophet rule or live. A degraded sensualism deprives this life of its grace and refinement; the next of its dignity and sanctity.
>
> The fact that in Mohammedan law every woman must belong to some man as his absolute property— either as a child, a wife, or a concubine—must delay the final extinction of slavery until the faith

of Islam has ceased to be a great power among men. Individual Moslems may show splendid qualities. Thousands become the brave and loyal soldiers of the Queen: all know how to die. But the influence of the religion paralyzes the social development of those who follow it. No stronger retrograde force exists in the world. Far from being moribund, Mohammedanism is a militant and proselytizing faith. It has already spread throughout central Africa, raising fearless warriors at every step; and were it not that Christianity is sheltered in the strong arms of science—the science against which it had vainly struggled—the civilization of modern Europe might fall, as fell the civilization of ancient Rome."

In the 1840's. **Alexis de Tocqueville** traveled twice to Algeria. He wrote to Arthur de Gobineau, October 22, 1843 (*Tocqueville Reader*, p. 229):

"I studied the Koran a great deal. I came away from that study with the conviction *there have been few religions in the world as deadly to men as that of Mohammed.*

...So far as I can see, it is the principle cause of the decadence so visible today in the Muslim world and, though less absurd than the polytheism of old, its social and political tendencies are in my opinion to be feared, and I therefore regard it as a form of decadence rather than a form of progress in relation to paganism itself."

In looking at these major belief systems and their views of God, we find tremendous diversity:

- Hindus acknowledge multitudes of gods and goddesses.
- Buddhists say there is no deity.
- New Age Spirituality (which is discussed in more detail later in this chapter) followers believe they are God.
- Muslims believe in a powerful but unknowable God.
- Christians believe in a loving God who created them to know him.

Are all religions worshiping the same God? Let's consider that. New Age Spirituality teaches that everyone should come to center on a cosmic consciousness, but it would require Islam to give up their one God, Hinduism to give up their numerous gods, and Buddhism to establish that there is a God. Of these, only one affirms that there is a loving God with whom one can be intimately acquainted.

A discussion of the major religions of the world would be incomplete without offering two other belief systems, both of which seem to be growing in the number of converts.

Secular Humanism

Writing for Free Inquiry, Tom Flynn, the executive director of the Council for Secular Humanism, defined his philosophy this way:

> Secular humanism begins with atheism (absence of belief in a deity) and agnosticism or skepticism (epistemological caution that rejects the transcendent as such due to a lack of evidence). Because no transcendent power will save us, secular humanists maintain that humans must take responsibility for

themselves. While atheism is a necessary condition for secular humanism, it is not a sufficient one. Far from living in a moral vacuum, secular humanists "wish to encourage wherever possible the growth of moral awareness and the capacity for free choice and an understanding of the consequences thereof."

Secular humanism emerges, then, as a comprehensive nonreligious life stance that incorporates a naturalistic philosophy, a cosmic outlook rooted in science, and a consequentialist ethical system. That is the definition I offer.

Flynn writes of the secular humanist agenda:

Secular humanism is a balanced and fulfilling life stance. It is more than atheism, more than "unhyphenated humanism;" it offers its own significant emergent qualities. The secular humanist agenda is a full one—in my opinion, an essential agenda for contemporary civilization. Surely it is more than enough to justify the existence of an independent organization dedicated to implementing it. The Council for Secular Humanism has a compelling mission, one we will continue to pursue with determination and vigor.

C. R. Hallpike, in his book entitled *Do We Need God to be Good* writes that humanists buy into the idea that one has to love himself before he can love anyone else. They place a lot of emphasis on self-esteem in the belief that if we could only eliminate the lack of esteem in which our children hold themselves, there is no limit to what they might accomplish.

The Self-Esteem Movement started in the United States in the 1970s because many psychiatrists and psychologists thought that the root of the majority of our problems was the absence of self-esteem. An eminent scholar, Nathaniel Branden wrote, "I cannot think of a single psychological problem—from anxiety and depression, to fear of intimacy or success, to spouse battering or of child molestation—that is not traceable to the problem of low self-esteem." Neil Smelser, formerly a professor of Sociology at the University of California, claimed, "Many, if not most of the major problems plaguing society have roots in the low self-esteem of many of the people who make up society."

By the late 1980s there was even a National Association for Self-Esteem. By golly, we were going to take this terrible problem head-on and remove that barrier to our children's learning.

A major problem seems to be that our American school-age children score much lower on basic standardized tests than do students from other developed (and some not-so-highly-developed!) nations in math, science and reading. The one thing in which our students excel is... self-esteem. We are right at the top (sixth) in that category. Hallpike identified two types of self-esteem: That which is an accurate reflection of one's worth as a person; a balanced, accurate appreciation of one's own successes and competencies—that's wonderful. However, there is also a type of self-esteem that produces an inflated, arrogant, unwarranted feeling of superiority unaccompanied by accomplishments, and that is another story. To tell a child how wonderful he is, for instance, at baseball when he can neither throw nor catch is a cruel lie which will be exposed by the slightest competition.

But, hey—people who have the latter kind of self-esteem can see themselves as gorgeous while onlookers may fail to see the basis of their confidence. The fact is. self-esteem must be earned before it can truly be of value to the holder.

Another quote from Hallpike's book reads, "Accurate self-knowledge would be more useful than high self-esteem in raising performance levels in all areas of one's life." That may be a gross understatement.

New Age

Here is a passage from Wikipedia describing New Ageism:

> New Age is a term applied to a range of spiritual or religious beliefs and practices that developed in Western nations during the 1970s. Precise scholarly definitions of the New Age differ in their emphasis, largely as a result of its highly eclectic structure. Although analytically often considered to be religious, those involved in New Age typically prefer the designation of Spiritual, as Mind, Body, Spirit, and rarely use the term "New Age" themselves. Many scholars of the subject refer to it as the New Age Movement, although others contest this term and suggest that it is better seen as a milieu or zeitgeist.
>
> As a form of Western esotericism, the New Age drew heavily upon a number of older esoteric traditions, in particular those that emerged from the occultist current that developed in the eighteenth century. Such prominent occult influences include the work of Emanuel Swedenborg and Franz Mesmer, as well as the ideas of Spiritualism, New Thought, and

Theosophy. A number of mid-twentieth century influences, such as the UFO religions of the 1950s, the Counterculture of the 1960s, and the Human Potential Movement, also exerted a strong influence on the early development of the New Age. The exact origins of the phenomenon remain contested, but there is general agreement that it developed in the 1970s, at which time it was centered largely in the United Kingdom. It expanded and grew more in the 1980s and 1990s, in particular within the United States. By the start of the 21st century, the term "New Age" was increasingly rejected within this milieu, with some scholars arguing that the New Age phenomenon had ended.

Despite its highly eclectic nature, a number of beliefs commonly found within the New Age have been identified. Theologically, the New Age typically adopts a belief in a holistic form of divinity that imbues all of the universe, including human beings themselves. There is thus a strong emphasis on the spiritual authority of the self. This is accompanied by a common belief in a wide variety of semi-divine non-human entities, such as angels and masters, with whom humans can communicate, particularly through the form of channeling. Typically viewing human history as being divided into a series of distinct ages, a common New Age belief is that whereas once humanity lived in an age of great technological advancement and spiritual wisdom, it has entered a period of spiritual degeneracy, which will be remedied through the establishment of a coming Age of Aquarius, from which the milieu gets its name. There is also a strong focus on healing, particularly using forms of alternative medicine, and an emphasis on a New Age "science" that seeks to unite science and spirituality.

Centered primarily in Western countries, those involved in the New Age have been primarily from middle and upper-middle-class backgrounds. The degree to which New Agers are involved in the milieu varied considerably, from those who adopted a number of New Age ideas and practices to those who fully embraced and dedicated their lives to it. The New Age has generated criticism from established Christian organizations as well as modern Pagan and indigenous communities. From the 1990s onward, the New Age became the subject of research by academic scholars of religious studies.

What exactly is *New Ageism*? Barbara Curtis, writing for Crosswalk.com (a subsidiary of Salem Web Network, an apparently non-denominational Christian network headquartered in Richmond, VA), says it is impossible to narrow down:

[T]he New Age is actually a vast smorgasbord of beliefs and practices. Each New Ager fills his tray with whatever assortment fits his appetite. All is liberally seasoned with self-centeredness. It's really a Have-It-Your-Way religion; thus its modern appeal.

Although there are many branches of New Age thought – ranging from meditation to fire-walking

– they stem from an ancient stock. The roots of the New Age tree spread around the globe to India. One might think that the desperate, degraded human condition of a land dominated by Hinduism would speak louder than words about the truth of the religion. But New Agers seem blind to the contradiction.

The typical New Ager believes:

- God is in everything (pantheism)
- All things are one (monism)
- Man is God
- Mind creates reality
- One's own experience validates the truth

Curtis writes that New Ageism is relativistic:

> New Agers do not believe in evil. Therefore, they do not accept man's problem as separation by sin from God. Instead, they believe that each of us has forgotten his or her own divinity. Therefore, the New Age solution is to seek "higher consciousness" through meditation, breathing exercises, yoga, diet, crystals, channeling, spirit guides, and more. Each of these diverse practices has the same purpose: to awaken the god in man.

The above items regarding the tenets of those religions were taken from official sites. I can add little to that discourse because I lack the requisite knowledge to comment further.

It is sobering that the admonitions of the Founders to follow Christian principles rather than looking to another religion, to philosophy or a set of tenets was accompanied by predictions of calamitous results should we not do so. It is not presented in the sense that it would be a good idea to follow the teachings of Christ in the application of law and in treating with one another, but rather that a democratic republic cannot survive unless the majority of its citizenry adhere to the teachings and precepts of Jesus Christ.

In his book, _Life at the Bottom,_ Theodore Dalrymple writes, "The idea that it is possible to base a society on no cultural or philosophical supposition at all, or alternatively, that all such presuppositions can be treated equally so that no choice has to be made between them, is absurd." _From the book, Life at the Bottom by Theodore Dalrymple, published in Great Britain by Ivan R. Dee, 2001._

Chapter 5

IS CULTURAL/MORAL EQUIVALENCY A REALITY?

Progressives/secular humanists do not like America—at least, not the America we were gifted with by the Founding Fathers. Why not? I haven't been able to figure that out yet. They apparently think that almost any mode of government and any culture of any other nation in the world is superior to that practiced in America. They have found the root of all the world's problems, and in their view, it is, unfortunately, America.

Are their cultures superior to ours?

In the *Conservative Review*, Walter Williams writes:

> There is little or no attention given by the mainstream media to the true cancer eating away at most of our institutions of higher learning. Philip Carl Salzman, emeritus professor of anthropology at McGill University, explains that cancer in a *Minding the Campus* article, titled "What Your Sons and Daughters Will Learn at University."
>
> Professor Salzman argues that for most of the 20th century, universities were dedicated to the

advancement of knowledge. There was open exchange and competition in the marketplace of ideas. Different opinions were argued and respected. Most notably, in the social sciences, social work, the humanities, education and law, this is no longer the case. Leftist political ideology has emerged. The most important thing to today's university communities is diversity of race, ethnicity, sex and economic class, on which they have spent billions of dollars. Conspicuously absent is diversity of ideology.

Students are taught that all cultural values are morally equivalent. That is ludicrous. Here are a few questions for those who make such a claim. Is forcible female genital mutilation, as practiced in nearly 30 sub-Saharan African and Middle Eastern countries, a morally equivalent cultural value? Slavery is currently practiced in Mauritania, Mali, Niger, Chad and Sudan; is it morally equivalent? In most of the Middle East, there are numerous limitations placed on women, such as prohibitions on driving, employment and education. Under Islamic law in some countries, female adulterers face death by stoning. Thieves face the punishment of having their hands severed. Homosexuality is a crime punishable by death in some countries. Are these cultural values morally equivalent, superior or inferior to Western values?

Social justice theory holds the vision that the world is divided between oppressors and victims. The theory holds that by their toxic masculinity, heterosexual white males are oppressors. Among their victims are females, people of color, and male and female homosexuals. The world's Christians and Jews are oppressors, and Muslims are victims.

For another look at moral equivalency, we turn to a piece from *American Thinker* entitled, "What I Learned in the Peace Corps in Africa: Trump is Right."

Karen McQuillan, now a well-known author, joined the Peace Corps, and just three weeks after graduating from college, she flew to Senegal, in western Africa to run a community center in a rural town. It was pretty slow living—no danger, except for her health, which was at considerable risk. When the urge to empty one's bowels hits the Senegalese, they take care of that problem—right there, and right then—even if it is in the middle of a busy street. As a result, there is fecal matter everywhere, and as it dries, it blows in the near-constant wind and is carried along in the very air you breathe. It is on you, on your clothing, on your food, and in your water.

She was warned the first day of training to not even touch water, because it would be contaminated by human feces, which carries parasites that bore through the skin and could even result in organ failure.

McQuillan said she was blown away when, a few decades after her Senegal experience, she began to see the liberals in the United States telling anyone who would listen that Western civilization was no better than the practices of third-world countries. Two entire generations of young people have been brainwashed into thinking it is wrong and racist to love your own culture and nation.

To Karen, Senegal is okay for Senegalese. They lived in filth but were unaware of the danger. They have a long-ingrained acceptance of corruption in politics. Theft as a way of life, and fidelity is a foreign concept to them. Women work like dogs all day while the men lounge under trees. The women often had to sell themselves to village men in order to earn enough money to feed and clothe their families. What was "blindingly obvious" to McQuillan was *these people are not the same as us.* They can be good, loving and kind, but the concept of right and wrong was not in their culture. It was not that they failed to follow the Ten Commandments—they were completely ignorant of them.

Corruption ruled in Senegal, from top to bottom. When a Senegalese got a job, they used it essentially for one purpose only—to steal anything that they could from their employer and give it to their "family," which might include as many as 100 people or more. Nobody seemed to understand that having a job meant you were supposed to work. In Senegal, the little stores were owned by Mauritanians. If a Senegalese wanted to run a store, he went to another country. Why? Because your friends and relatives would ask you for stuff for free, and you would have to give it to them. You were not allowed to be selfish and say no to relatives. There goes the business!

McQuillan believes that there are many intelligent, capable people in Senegal and perhaps someday they will understand and solve their own problems—on their terms, though—not ours. The solution is certainly not to bring thousands of Senegalese here to America.

Are all cultures equal? Would it be easy for someone from Senegal, for instance, to make his home in America and be a contributing, happy citizen? Sure, he could do it.

But...

Only if he decided that the country he came to was better than the one he left; in any event, was not Senegal, and then did his best to assimilate into his new country. If he would follow the laws of the United States, accept the work ethic of the American people, learn to make an effort to fit in rather than trying to change America to be like Senegal, he could make it. Anyone who thinks this would be easy need only go back a few paragraphs and read what the Peace Corps volunteer who spent three years in that country had to say. There are vast cultural differences, and anyone promoting a flood of Senegalese into American cities would be doing a grave disservice to both Senegalese and Americans.

How would a Palestinian, for instance, fit into a typical American city? I'm not talking about New York or Washington, D C—a real American city, in a real American school?

From Townhall.com:

> Palestinian children dressed as terrorists and staged a mock raid on Israelis as part of a Kindergarten graduation ceremony in Gaza City. The enactment even included a drone, weapons, and body cameras. Adoring relatives can be seen in the audience filming.
>
> Video footage of the event, which took place last year (2018), was posted on *The Daily Mail*. It shows five kids dressed like terror group Palestinian Islamic Jihad carrying mock sniper rifles and semi-automatic weapons as they raid a building. Inside are two other kids, one in Israeli civilian clothing and the other dressed as an Israeli soldier. Both are shown being captured.

I do not know whether that simulated raid conducted by kindergartners was held in a Mosque Madrasa—many Madrasas *are* located in Mosques. Contrast that action with what you might typically hear in a Christian church kindergarten Sunday School class, where children might be heard singing, *"Jesus loves the little children/ All the children of the world/Red and yellow, black and white/They are precious in his sight/Jesus loves the little children of the world."*

In which religious school would you rather your children or grandchildren participate?

Chapter 6

WHAT IS CHRISTIANITY?

Of all the systems of morality, ancient or modern which have come under my observation, none appears to me so pure as that of Jesus. —**Thomas Jefferson**

The Significance of Christianity

HISTORY IS VERY informative—which is why many of us cannot imagine the disinterest now shown in that subject in many of our public schools. It is from history that we learn how many/ most early governments were formed by strong men who gained suzerainty by force of arms and maintained control only for as long as they had sufficient forces to put down the occasional rebellion and stifle dissent among the citizenry. To most of the poor in the old feudal system, it made very little difference who was in control, their condition remained much the same. They worked long hours to produce for the manor lord and were allowed to keep only that portion necessary for their family to survive—if barely. Personal liberty was veritably unknown. Even if the very poor happened to possess a skill with which he might earn a living, it was rare that he was allowed into the ranks of the tradesman. He was destined for poverty his entire life and had nothing more to offer his progeny. If I have drawn a bleak picture of life in the Middle Ages, it's only because that is the way things were. But such conditions actually held from the beginning of civilization until well into the mid-1800s, that's how recently in human history it's been that most classes of people have been able to have a general expectation of material prosperity.

The birth of Christ was a momentous event, principally because it changed man's relationship with God forever. Individual lives for Christians were made not only bearable, but enjoyable, although in most instances the financial and living conditions for most Christians changed very little. That is not to say that the rich and powerful were not included among the number of those whose lives changed upon meeting Jesus Christ; the lives of the wealthy, too, were turned upside down, and they were never the same after their acceptance of Christ as Savior. But the Christian influence upon the governments of the world was slow-moving. Part of that might have been due to the admonition of Christ himself that we were to "render unto Caesar that which is Caesar's, and unto God that which is God's," clearly demonstrating a vast cleavage between the two kingdoms: earthly and spiritual. It is also inescapable that Jesus placed very little emphasis on worldly things, like comfort and wealth. The things that one might purchase with money meant very little to the Savior. It makes sense that his sincere followers "laid up for themselves heavenly treasure," rather than seeking the riches of the world.

This is certainly not to say that there were not spiritual, caring people in positions of leadership in governments of the ancient and medieval worlds. History records many events wherein kings, governors, lords, earls, etc. were generous and caring toward their subjects. But it would be an error to say that was the norm.

You see, New Age spiritualists and secular humanists (is there a real difference?) hold that man does not need a "god," because he is a god unto himself. They believe that man is good and getting better day-by-day. All elements necessary to live a complete life are wrapped up in the mind of man—he needs no spiritual being. And the humanist is convinced that there is no proof that prayer and supplications to a non-existent "god" have ever been efficacious.

Even if everything they needed for daily living was contained within the mind of man, I have not seen evidence in their dogma of a plan that would suffice for that individual of limited mental capacity. How would *he* be able to "live a complete life?" And if he is a god unto himself, would he not at best be a vastly inferior god?

Is man, or *humanity,* good in and of itself, and is human behavior truly getting better day-by-day? Just hearing the bizarre allegations and accusations people (politicians, especially) hurl at each other, such as, "Republicans *want* children and old people to die," makes one wonder whether there is *any* good in someone who thinks that way.

The first time I heard that remark, that "Republicans want children to die," I was stunned. Al Gore was the first person I heard utter that ridiculous statement, but he certainly wasn't the last. What kind of man would make such a horrid accusation about another human being? Most likely, Al Gore didn't mean that literally. That fact, however, was not in evidence by the look of utter hatred in his eyes at the moment he said it. Are we, the viewer and reader, to assume that when we hear or read of someone making such inflammatory remarks that this is merely hyperbole, and disregard what the person said? How about someone who is not blessed with a sophisticated understanding of the exaggerations that have become the stock–in-trade of many politicians? Is it necessary to paint our opponents as worse than the former Nazi or communist leaders who have killed millions of their own citizens in order to be elected to an office? If that is what it takes to win an election, may God have mercy on us all.

How can one read or watch the news and not have some doubt as to the goodness of man and his dealings with other human beings? Doubt must creep into the minds of the most devoted secularist as to the efficacy of their belief that each man is his own god, that he is innately good and thus has no need for any other deity.

That surely contrasts with the teachings of Jesus. The Bible teaches that man is fallen. He is born into sin and has no ability within himself to ever earn his own salvation. That *genuine evil* truly exists in the world, and that evil can reside within each of us—whether Christian or not. Yes, a Christian retains within himself a nature that can lead him into sins and wrongs as terrible as those acts committed by the vilest of men.

The difference is that the Christian has within his soul the presence of the Holy Spirit, the "earnest" of his salvation. The moment one accepts Christ as Lord and Savior, that Holy Spirit comes to reside in him—readily available to help the Christian to serve God.

Man has always had a free will—he can choose to serve God, or he can choose to live only for himself. God is never going to make that decision for him. He might provide that man with strong inferences of what He wishes that man might do, but the decision as to whether to follow the will of God is up to each person. Indeed, the only way that anyone can please God is to allow himself to be guided by God's Holy Spirit; to do as the Apostle Paul admonished and "die to self and live unto God."

I am sure that many non-Christians have a difficult time understanding what is meant by the term, "die to self." It cannot be fully grasped until one accepts that the Kingdom of God is not of this world. The finite mind of many men can conceive of the world only in what it sees and feels. All things must pass a certain degree of scientific muster before they can attain a level of believability.

Jesus told Pontius Pilate and many, many others that His was a *spiritual* kingdom, and that anyone who accepted Christ came to Him, "in spirit and in truth." But, while the Kingdom of God is not of this world, it possesses the perfect formula for living this earthly life in preparation for the life that is to come—that everlasting life of which Jesus often spoke.

One of the distressing things taught and practiced by secular humanists is the concept of moral equivalency—that one religion, one philosophy, one system of beliefs is just as good as any other. Former President Obama not only denied that America was or ever had been a Christian nation, but often postulated that Islam is a beautiful religion that has as much to offer its practitioners as does Christianity.

Really?

I am no aficionado of Islam or the Quran, but a book and/ or religion which informs its readers that they should kill all infidels (those who do not follow the beliefs of Islam) is not as "user-friendly" as is the Christian Bible, where the admonition is to "Do good to them who spitefully use you." Apologists for Islam assure us that these verses urging murder of infidels are 'taken out of context'. Perhaps that is so. The Quran also teaches that if you turn your back on Allah, Allah ceases to love you. The Bible teaches that God loves the sinner as well as the saint; whether or not you love Him. The Bible teaches that the only way to be pleasing to God is to "love one another." In one place, Jesus tells His disciples to "Love thy neighbor."

When one of His Jewish followers asked Him the question, "Lord, who is our neighbor?" Jesus launched into one of the more revealing parables in the Bible.

He recounted the story of the Jewish traveler who was beset on the road by robbers, who beat him, robbed him and left him for dead. Two Jewish religious leaders, one of them a temple priest, the other a member of the tribe of Levi, the tribe of priests of which all temple priests were a part, came by, saw the man and "passed by on the other side," walking over to the other side of the road so that they would not have to look upon the poor unfortunate victim.

Then, along came a Samaritan—a hated foreigner that practicing Jews would refuse to associate with. Jesus told His disciples that the Samaritan gave the man a drink, bound up his wounds, and took him to an inn. The Samaritan told the innkeeper to care for the man and nurture him back to health. He gave the innkeeper money and promised that if he spent more on the injured man, then he (the Samaritan) would repay him when he came back on his return trip.

Then Jesus asked the question, "Who, then, was the traveler's neighbor?"

The Gospel of Christ is for everyone—Jew or gentile (to the Jew, a "gentile" is anyone of any origin other than Jewish). The Christian is admonished to be about the business of spreading the gospel of Jesus Christ "in Judea, Samaria and to the ends of the earth." Muslims will tell you they are about the same task. The method of conversion utilized by Christians must be gentle persuasion, under the leadership of the Holy Spirit. The laws embraced by Christians are more geared to reform rather than any element of force. It encourages the lawbreaker and persuades him to mend his errant ways.

It is precisely because of this teaching of love for one another and consideration for the rights and well-being of others that Christianity was perceived—correctly, we believe—to be the only religion that could possibly work to sustain the liberties and freedoms promised by the American Constitution. Because it had proven itself to be good and just.

The Founders thought it unlikely that Americans would ever depart from the "good news of the Gospel of Jesus Christ."

Accepting Christ and Knowing His Will

Thomas Jefferson said, "Christianity is the best friend of government because it is the only religion that changes the heart."

Yes, when practiced as Jesus taught it, Christianity changes an undisciplined, prideful, greedy, inconsiderate heart into one that loves Jesus, and through Him, all of mankind. All it takes is a decision to accept Christ's love and live in it.

God is omnipotent (above all in authority), omniscient (knowledgeable of all things), omnipresent (everywhere at once), immutable (never changing), and perfect (in Him is no sin). Despite all this, He cannot be seen. That may cause you to think that He cannot be close to you; that He cannot love or comfort you. Nothing could be further from the truth.

To draw from personal experience, when I was much younger, not long after I invited Christ into my heart, I began to feel that I should enter the ministry and become a preacher of God's gospel. Even now, many years later, I believe the Holy Spirit impressed this upon me. While much time has passed since then, I still recall the relationship that I had with God during those early years of being a Christian. I could maintain a prayerful attitude all day long—on my walk to school, while sitting in class, while practicing football, and even (maybe especially) when I rode a bucking horse in rodeos (I never did get over being afraid!).

I never felt out of touch with my Savior. I knew that He cared for me such that even my smallest concerns were heard. It may seem strange, but I was not as concerned with whether God answered my prayers as I was that I would recognize his answers. This meant being attuned to his will and being ready to follow it, even if it were directly opposite of what I had hoped for or desired to have happen. For my real desire was to be a willing and eager instrument in God's hands.

How did I know what God would have me do?

How do you know what *anybody* tells you? I'm not trying to sow mistrust in you—nothing of the sort. Let me simply ask, do you believe *everything* that anybody tells you? No? Then how much do you believe, and what is your filtering system for making such a determination?

Do you just let sound waves hit your ear drum, or is more involved in the art of listening?

Real listening requires that we "listen" with our eyes. While we certainly hear one's words, we are also looking at the eyes to see whether they agree with the mouth. Or we see the face or neck blush, or arms crossed in front as though shutting you out. No, there is more to understanding what a person is saying than simply listening to the words.

When we listen to God, we listen with the heart and soul. I have never heard the voice of God aloud, yet I am often as certain of His direction in my life as if He *had* spoken to me directly. Just as we must be attentive in human conversation, we must have our mind and soul in unison with God in order to receive what He is trying to reveal to us. Of course, God does not guard the truth like a suspected criminal might. He has a clear, direct channel to our thinking, so when we fail to apprehend His meaning, it is our fault. I heard a man say once that if you find yourself distant from God, you can be sure that it wasn't God who moved.

If you can navigate the noise of the material world and focus on God's will, it can be the source of discipline and humility. Thinking back over my life, I recall moments in which God answered my prayers in ways that almost seemed to subvert my own will—in what always turned out to be far better outcome than that for which I had asked. For years, I would be surprised when He instructed me to address the condition that had prompted my prayer in the first place. You see, I would often ask God to intervene in situations where I felt something needed to be done, but I felt completely ill-equipped and inadequate to do it. In essence, my prayer was that God find a different person for the task at hand—someone with the skills and talents to do the job well.

Something that has taken me many years to grasp (and I still struggle with) is that God does not necessarily find the person with the ready-made abilities and talents to accomplish His will. He would rather empower the person He chooses to accomplish the task.

How does God empower the people He selects for certain tasks? I can only answer that question in a personal way, by telling of how God enabled me to do things that I was incapable of doing.

I used to sing. I'd sing loudly in the shower, alone in my FBI car, and occasionally in church.

Have you ever heard your own voice on a taped recording? The first time I heard my own recorded voice, I thought that awful sound belonged to a pig caught in a fence or some poor fellow who was being tortured and screaming for help. I was shocked! If I sounded like that to the congregation, why were they not pelting me with overripe tomatoes and other garbage? I hoped my singing didn't sound the same to them. Otherwise, I might be subject to prosecution for cruel and inhumane punishment.

This is embarrassing to say, but there have been times when I heard my voice live and thought it sounded rather pleasant. In those moments, I believed that I actually could sing. This was particularly true when I was accompanied on the piano by my beautiful daughter, Kim, who had the keenest sense of timing and dynamics of any accompanist with whom I have ever sung. She knew when to speed the song up and when to slow it down. She knew how to play *pianissimo* when the lyrics of the song bespoke reverence and intimacy and when to play *fortissimo* when the music reflected on the power and majesty of God—a wonderful pianist!

I noticed on those occasions when I spent time polishing a song to suit my particular vocal strengths rather than praying that it would reflect the love and grace of Jesus, the result was terrible, embarrassing—a complete flop. Every time! Let me share a story with you that hopefully will explain why I think this is the case and the significance of it.

In the early seventies, while I was assigned to the Berkeley Resident Agency of the FBI, the Billy Graham Evangelistic Crusade visited Oakland, California. Oakland abutted Berkeley on the south. Our senior Agent in Berkeley, Don Jones, had met Billy Graham and the entire Crusade team years earlier at a crusade in Jones' home state of Ohio. In fact, Don had served as a sort of bodyguard for Reverend Graham.

Don asked me to accompany him one day to meet George Beverly Shea for lunch at the hotel where the team was staying, just south of Oakland. Shea was a long-time Crusade member—perhaps going back to the very beginning—and a wonderful singer. That luncheon was a most interesting experience. Bev, as Don Jones called him (I didn't have the nerve to call him that) was as humble, kind, and gracious as anyone you have ever met.

While we were eating lunch, a young woman approached our table. She had a guitar in her hands, and I learned that she was a recording artist who had been invited to sing at the Crusade service that evening. She played a couple bars of the song she intended to sing and asked Mr. Shea's advice as to how she should end the piece. She could take it to a high crescendo that probably showed her voice off at its very best, or she could do it as the songwriter had written it. It was obvious which *she* would rather do.

Instead of answering her directly, Mr. Shea told the story of a songwriter who had written a number especially for him. Those of you old enough might recall that George Beverly Shea had a deep voice; he could knock the bottom out of the bass register. This song for some reason was not written that way. However, everyone who heard him practice it speculated how impressive it might sound if he took a low note at the end of the song, rather than singing it the way it had been written.

Mr. Shea said, "I asked myself—if I did the song that way (taking the 'low road'), would I be doing it for Jesus' glory, or for my own?" He shook his head. "I just couldn't do it."

I don't recall how the young lady sang her song that night, but I would bet that she did not hit that extra high note.

These stories illustrate how one's potential is constrained by his motives if they aren't God-centered. They also demonstrate how God empowers us to do things that are beyond our human capabilities.

In this, my beliefs may differ from those of many other evangelicals. I believe that at the moment we become a Christian—the moment we confess our sins, acknowledge Jesus Christ as our Lord and Savior, and welcome Him into our heart—we are 'in-dwelt' by the Holy Spirit. If you get tired of reading that, I apologize. It is, however, that important.

Man, that's heavy. What does it mean to be 'indwelt' by the Holy Spirit?

In Chapter 14, verse 49 of his gospel, Luke records Jesus saying to His apostles and other followers, "And, Behold, I send the promise of my Father upon you; but tarry ye in the city of Jerusalem, until ye be endued with power from on high."

In John 14:15-19, Jesus said to His disciples:

> If ye love me, keep my commandments. And I will
> pray the Father, and He shall give you another
> Comforter, that He may abide with you forever;
> Even the Spirit of truth, whom the world cannot
> receive because it seeth Him not, neither knoweth
> Him: but ye know Him; for he dwelleth with you,
> and *shall be in you.* I will not leave you comfortless;
> I will come to you. Yet a little while, and the world

seeth me no more; but ye see me, because I live, ye
shall live also (New Schofield Reference Bible).

The fulfillment of that promise made in Luke's 14th chapter is
recorded in John 20:19–22:

> Then the same day at evening, being the first day of
> the week, when the doors were shut where the apos-
> tles were assembled for fear of the Jews, came Jesus
> and stood in the midst, and saith unto them, 'Peace
> be unto you.' And when He had so said, He showed
> unto them His hands, and His side. Then were the
> disciples glad when they saw the Lord. Then said
> Jesus unto them again, 'Peace be unto you; as my
> Father hath sent me, even so send I you.' And when
> He had said this, He breathed on them, and saith
> unto them, 'Receive ye the Holy Spirit'.

The Apostle Paul, in writing to the church at Corinth, said in 2
Corinthians 1:21-22:

> "Now, He who establisheth us with you in Christ,
> and hath anointed us, is God. Who hath also sealed
> us, and given the earnest of the (Holy) Spirit in
> our hearts."

Another place in scripture where Jesus tells His disciples a little
bit about the Holy Spirit is John 16:12-13:

> I have yet many things to say unto you, but ye
> cannot bear them now. Nevertheless, when He, the
> Spirit of truth is come, he will guide you into all

truth, for he shall not speak of himself, but whatever he shall hear, that shall he speak; and he shall show you things to come. He shall glorify me, for he shall receive of mine, and shall show it unto you."

I offer just a few more verses where the Bible speaks about the Holy Spirit. Please, look them up: Galatians 4:6; Romans 8:9; Romans 8:11.

The Holy Spirit has many responsibilities, but one of the principal jobs He performs is to guide us into all truths regarding Jesus Christ and to lead us to an understanding of God's will for our lives. How does He do this? I will explain for readers who want to share the Gospel, and maybe, some who might be intrigued by Christianity.

Being Transformed, or "Born Again"

Those readers who have never had the privilege of testifying in a criminal case at court will at least have watched a court scene in a movie or on TV. If so, you may be familiar with the phrase, *rules of evidence.* One rule of evidence is that you can only testify to those things that you have seen with your own eyes or heard with your own ears. To say in court, "John told me that he heard Jake say he robbed a bank" violates that rule. You would be testifying to "hearsay," which is unacceptable without the judge's permission.

When a Christian speaks of *witnessing,* he is talking about sharing his salvation experience with an interested party who has yet to accept Christ as Savior. In so doing, the witness is sharing his very own encounter with the Lord—not that of another Christian, but his own experience. Thus, the term *witness* applies to that sharer because it does not involve hearsay.

In this tradition, I offer another story:

I have already told you about the feeling that I had been called by God to preach. I was also once invited to "bring the message" at a nearby rural church for both Sunday morning and evening services.

When I say the church was rural, full disclosure requires that I remind you that the metropolis where I grew up and went to school had a sign at the north edge of town that read: Pop. 2,212. Everything is relative, you see.

I was a young man recently surrendered to the ministry of preaching the Gospel of Jesus Christ, and this was one of my first opportunities to do so. I intended to take full advantage. I had prepared a sermon that would leave a lasting impression on the lucky audience, one that would make them realize, "Now, this is a guy who can *preach*! He's going somewhere." I worked all week on the two sermons, referring more to the dictionary than to the Bible (BIG mistake). Too often, a big word I wanted to use meant something other than what I thought.

I was so excited that Sunday morning as I pulled up to the church. I could hardly wait for the song service and the time of offering (money for the expenses of the church) to end so that I could get up behind that pulpit and begin to preach.

I had never seen—*you* have never seen—people less impressed, less awed, or more bored.

A speaker once said he did not mind when people occasionally looked at their watches while he was speaking. He said it was when they began to shake them, as if they thought their watches had stopped, that he knew he was in trouble.

I knew I had made a grave mistake before I had even finished the first of my three points. I stumbled on, but I wanted to run from that church and never come back. Even though I cut the sermon short, it still seemed interminably long. As bad as it was for the congregation, it was miserable for me.

Eventually the service concluded, and after the closing hymn, I headed for the exit. Such was my shame for what I had done that part of me wanted the chairman of the deacons to call after me and say, "We won't be needing you to come back tonight."

What did I do that was so awful besides making a fool of myself?

I went into that church with the idea of impressing the members with *my* talents and abilities—not to share with them the grace and love of Jesus Christ. It was a betrayal of the trust that God had given me. I had let down my audience, but my worse sin was letting down my Lord. A preacher of the Gospel is to hide himself behind the cross of Christ, not stand before it. Had I spent half the time in prayer that I had used in looking up impressive words, mine might have been an acceptable sermon. Had I only allowed the Holy Spirit, who dwells within me, to be my guide.

I cried all the way home. When I got there, I didn't speak to my parents. I went to my bedroom and lay down across the bed. I wanted to die.

How do you recover from something so devastating?

I had prepared another "stem-winder" of a message to present to the church that evening, but I did not even want to face the parishioners who had seen my petty pride and pitiful attempt to impress them. They undoubtedly had seen right through me to my true motives that morning. What was I going to do?

It gave me some comfort, at least, to know that many of them who had heard the first message would not be back for a second helping in the evening services. When I was finished crying, although still thoroughly ashamed of myself, I thought, *What am I going to do tonight? I can't use the message I prepared. They'll throw me right out of their church—and rightly so.*

I opened my Bible and pointed with my finger to a place on the facing page. I really cannot remember what verse in the New Testament my finger fell upon (after all, that was more than 65 years ago!) but I do recall an overwhelming impression, a feeling, an urging—call it what you will—that my message should be built around that verse. I know as well as I know I am sitting here now that it was the Holy Spirit reassuring me that I was not abandoned, and that if I would allow Him, He would help me put together a sermon that would glorify Christ.

I began to relax as I stopped worrying about what I would say, and in less than an hour I was prepared for my evening visit to the church.

I didn't *glad hand* the members as I came in. I probably should have apologized for that morning's message, but all I could think about was the words of an old Christian hymn that I had sung many times, "Turn your eyes upon Jesus." At that moment, those words meant more to me than ever before. I was praying that the Holy Spirit would fill me and enable me to focus our attention on Jesus.

Was it a great sermon? No. I never delivered one of those. But when it was finished, I knew that I had at least done what God would have had me do. God had blessed my effort, as feeble as it was, and that was enough.

Would that I could say I had learned that lesson once and forever.

It didn't happen. It doesn't happen. As the Bible teaches, man is fallen. He is born in sin and has no ability within himself to ever earn his own salvation. While a Christian establishes a new spiritual being within himself when he accepts Christ, he yet retains a nature that can lead him into sin. Romans 3:23 says, "For all have sinned and fall short of the glory of God." That's you. It's certainly me. And that includes all of mankind.

By giving the Holy Spirit control of our lives, words and actions, we can resist our broken nature. That's good news. However, to some, the idea of relinquishing sinful pleasures can be a huge stumbling block.

George Bernard Shaw, a professed atheist, once said he would not be a Christian because of all the things he would have to give up should he convert. And he wanted to do what he wanted to do.

That is the way most non-Christians look at it. Their mind is set on all the things they love that they would have to forsake. A Christian can only marvel when he hears someone express such feelings.

What of value does one have to give up?

Well, really... Nothing!

At the University of California in Berkeley, a man of my acquaintance who had a doctorate in mathematics, an atheist we'll call Robert, became a Christian through the life example and patient explanations of a fellow professor we'll call Marty. Robert had enjoyed drinking for most of his adult life. After he accepted Jesus as his personal savior, he told Marty that he saw no reason to quit drinking. If the small church of which Marty was a member would not accept that, then he didn't want to join the church. Marty told Robert, "As long as you see nothing wrong with drinking beer, by all means continue." Robert did start attending the church and did continue drinking beer at home and in bars with his friends. To my knowledge, nobody in the church said anything to him about this.

However, in about a month to six weeks, Robert told Marty, "You know, I just don't feel comfortable with my bar friends anymore. I mean, I still like those guys, but the things they talk most about are no longer interesting to me. They sound sort of cheap and childish. I feel a lot freer at the church, among my church friends."

Robert paused for a few moments. "I didn't think this would ever happen, but I don't feel right about drinking beer anymore. And surprisingly, I don't miss the bars or the beer."

Nobody should ever quit an activity he has enjoyed for years just on the say-so of another person. That person's reasoning may not be correct or even rational. The only thing that should cause one to change once they become a Christian is the influence of God's Holy Spirit. If Christ has truly taken up residence in the heart and soul, as should happen upon conversion, one will not wish to continue behaviors that are not pleasing in God's sight. If the Holy Spirit does not convict one in that regard, then they should not alter their actions.

Those who remain skeptical of Christianity because they want to maintain their current lifestyle should remember that God knows better than anyone what is good for them. Do you really believe that you would have to give up much in life that is enjoyable to serve a God who loved you so much? It is because of that great love He has for you that He wants the very best for you, not the worst. This human weakness, the reluctance to sacrifice superficial pleasures for what is truly good, is captured in this quote by C.S. Lewis from an address called *The Weight of Glory* :

> It would seem that Our Lord finds our desires not too strong, but too weak. We are half-hearted creatures, fooling about with drink and sex and ambition when infinite joy is offered us, like an ignorant child who wants to go on making mud pies in a slum because he cannot imagine what is meant by the offer of a holiday at the sea. We are far too easily pleased.

Hopefully, these stories demonstrate a part of the role of the Holy Spirit. Their common themes may even be useful to an understanding of how to become a Christian. All one needs to do is accept that you are a sinner, confess to that, repent of your sins, and humbly ask Jesus Christ to come into your heart and save you—to be your Savior, Lord, and the Master of your life. That's it.

Obstacles to Faith

The Gospel of Christ is not difficult to understand. The fact is, the very simplicity of God's message is one of the great barriers for people who either really are or perceive themselves to be intellectually superior. Surely, a God so mighty, so majestic, so infinite in wisdom cannot have conceived an idea for saving His people that is so ridiculously simple? On his Crusades, Reverend Billy Graham put the plan of salvation simply: "Believe on the Lord Jesus Christ and you will be saved."

The simplicity of Christ's plan is also noted by Thomas Jefferson, a renowned intellectual, who wrote, "The doctrines of Jesus are simple, and tend to the happiness of man."

Theologians often try to make the Gospel complicated, adding many things one must do in addition to accepting Christ as your Savior, much like the Sadducees and Pharisees made Judaism impossible to follow. But recall what Jesus said in Matthew 19:14, "Let the children come to me, and do not hinder them, for to such belongs the kingdom of heaven."

I prefer the wording of the Kings James Bible, wherein Jesus says, "Suffer little children, and forbid them not, to come unto me; for of such is the kingdom of heaven. And He laid His hands upon them and went away."

Children sense love in a way that adults do not. You can tell a child you love him or her, but that child has an intuitive ability to see in your face and your actions whether this is true. In many ways, it is more difficult to fool a child than it is to hoodwink a member of Mensa.

It is worth noting that Jesus' own disciples were discouraging people from bringing their children to Jesus for a blessing. That prompted Jesus' reply recorded here. Also, in Matthew 18:3, Jesus said, "Verily I say unto you, except ye be converted, and become as little children, ye shall not enter the kingdom of heaven."

What did Jesus mean by that?

Many years ago, while we were swimming off a dock in a beautiful clear lake, three of us who were fathers began calling for our small children to jump off the dock and into our arms. The water was probably 15 feet deep. Surprisingly, our daughter, Kim, who was two years old at that time, just leapt right to me. To tell you the truth, it frightened me a little. I was concerned that I wouldn't be able to keep her above the water so that she wouldn't become afraid—or, far worse, drown! She had more faith in me than I had in myself.

I think Jesus asks us for the kind of faith that my daughter had in me that day. The difference is, there is no trepidation in the heart of Jesus. He is mighty to save, and all that is required of us is to take that leap of faith into His loving arms. By His grace He has already secured our atonement. In a way, He is asking us to demonstrate the faith of a child—not the nagging doubt of a mature hearer of the Word.

Upon reflection, it should make sense that God's plan should be as simple as it is. Would a God who created the entire universe (and perhaps many other universes besides the one we occupy) have *need* of an intelligent man or woman to instruct His people? By no means! Anyone should be able to spread the Gospel. If God calls you to perform a task for Him, He will equip you perfectly for the job. All that you need to accomplish His will is *willingness*.

Chapter 7

AMERICA IS GREAT BECAUSE AMERICA IS GOOD

ALEXIS DE TOCQUEVILLE, a French aristocrat, born July 29, 1805 in Paris, France, visited the United States in 1831. The original purpose of his visit was to study American prisons. Upon seeing the American experiment with a Democratic Republic, he became curious as to why the American experience with that form of governance turned out so well for them, while the French attempt with the same form of government went horribly wrong. The book he wrote, *Democracy in America*, recounting his stay in that nation is slightly stilted and not easy to follow. However, there were some gems of truth in what he wrote that are well worth mining.

Tocqueville was later the French Foreign Minister in 1849, and died in Cannes, France in 1859 at the age of 53.

Americans found in Tocqueville their trustworthy European supporter of democracy, without the British-style censorings but insightful agreements and serious criticisms.

Democracy in America was perhaps one of the first theoretical publications on American exceptionalism. According to Seymour Martin Lipset, perhaps the best known and still most influential work of the "foreign traveler literatures" is Tocqueville's *Democracy in America*.

In his great book, Tocqueville is the first to refer to the United States as exceptional—that is, qualitatively different from all other countries. He is, therefore, the initiator of the writings on American exceptionalism.

In the introduction to *Land Without Ghosts: Chinese Impressions of America from the Mid-Nineteenth to the Present,* R. David Arkush and Leo O. Lee remark on differences noticed by Europeans such as Tocqueville between American society and their monarchial system.

> Visitors from the old world were astonished... when waiters, hotel chambermaids and train conductors unselfconsciously engaged them in casual conversation, asking direct questions, and plainly showing that they considered themselves as good as anyone else.

Naturally European commentary emphasized American egalitarianism, and observations often led to hyperbolic visions of America as a classless society.

Mostly writing for a French audience, Tocqueville wrote:

> If, after a lengthy period of observation and sincere meditation, people were to become convinced that the gradual and progressive development of equality was at once a part of their future, the process would immediately take on a sacred character, as it were an expression of the sovereign master's will. *To wish to arrest democracy would then seem tantamount to a struggle against God himself.*

The most famous and often repeated line from Tocqueville's book, that, "America is great because America is good," is apparently something Tocqueville never actually said. So, where did that saying—quoted by people with such diverse viewpoints as Ronald Reagan, Charles Colson and Bill Clinton—come from?

What did Tocqueville say about the aspect of American goodness?

He did say that there is to be found in America the spirit of faith, closely intertwined with the spirit of freedom, to produce a country that was more enlightened than any European nation and the freest country in the world. He said America was a nation where "the Christian religion has kept the greatest real power over men's souls." What he seems to be saying is that democratic republics need religion, and more specifically, the *Christian religion,* in order to survive and thrive.

Tocqueville also observed, "The people rule in the political realm as God rules in the universe," applying the same directives to do that which is right and good. He fully understood that the liberties provided by the Constitution and the Bill of Rights were almost a temptation to potential abusers of those rights. While he was adamantly opposed to the slavery practiced in the southern states, the temptation to deny people certain of their rights was offset by a desire to treat others well. He wrote:

> In my opinion, the main evil of the present democratic institutions of the United States does not arise from their weakness, but from their strength... I am not so much alarmed at the excessive liberty which reigns in that country as at the inadequate securities which one finds there against tyranny.

Alexander Hamilton might have said, join the club. There is no question that was a real concern for the country's ability to fend off the trend toward despotism or tyranny without stronger safeguards being built into the Constitution, giving the young republic the power to defend itself against the *forces of evil*.

Why had the United States not succumbed to the willfulness of ordinary men and sunk into one of those conditions Tocqueville so feared? He believed the safeguard was no more than the *habits of restraint* that had been inculcated into the American people until it became second nature, reminding them that while you have the right to do almost anything, many of those things are not good for you and can be very damaging to society as a whole. As British Conservative Benjamin Disraeli said, "Next to knowing when to seize an opportunity, the most important thing in life is to know when to forego an advantage."

America's religious beliefs were very much a part of their habit of restraint. *"In the United States,"* Tocqueville wrote, *"Christianity reigns without obstacle."* Many would say, "Wouldn't it be wonderful if the same situation obtained today." Americans had learned that denying themselves a short-term pleasure often made for a better long-term result. This kind of thinking helped to develop "a multitude of citizens who are disciplined, moderate, prudent and self-controlled." So, while "the law allows them to do everything, there are things which religion (Christianity) prevents them from imagining and forbids them to dare."

The Frenchman also said, although "religion... never intervenes directly in the government of American Society," it nevertheless functions as "the first of their political institutions." If Christianity did not give Americans their taste for liberty, "it does notably facilitate their use of that liberty."

I believe that when Tocqueville said Americans are good, he was speaking in a moral, ethical and spiritual sense. It is the goodness in them, the love and respect that they have for each other, the honesty that attends, or should attend, all of their business dealings, that is the kind of "good" to which he made reference:

> In the United States hardly anybody talks of the beauty of virtue, but they maintain that virtue is useful and prove it every day. The American moralists do not profess that men ought to sacrifice themselves for their fellow creatures because it is noble to make such sacrifices, but they boldly aver that such sacrifices are as necessary to him *who imposes them upon himself* as to him for whose sake they are made.

That is Christian love in action.

> They have found out, in their country and their age, man is brought home to himself by an irresistible force; and, losing all hope of stopping that force, they turn all their thoughts to the direction of it. They therefore do not deny that every man may follow his own interest, but they endeavor to prove that it is in the best interest of every man to be virtuous. I shall not here enter into the reasons they allege, which would divert me from my subject; suffice to say that they have convinced their fellow countrymen.

Again, that *virtue* is another example of Christian love in action; an indication of the good in the American people.

A young man of my acquaintance was a sales representative for a large corporation. He was on his way to make a few cold calls; not by phone, but visiting offices without an appointment to leave his card and put the name of his product in front of prospective buyers.

It was a cold, rainy morning with a brisk north breeze as the salesman left his home and drove toward the interstate highway which was the main north-south artery in the Oklahoma City area. As he took the on-ramp and began picking up speed, he noticed an elderly woman standing at the side of the ramp. She had on an old heavy coat and a felt-looking hat, both already drenched. By her feet was a small, battered suitcase. He was already past her before he had processed all this information, but he pulled over and stopped the car. He ran back to ask the elderly lady if she wanted a ride. She nodded. The man picked up her suitcase, walked with her to his car, opened the door so that she could get into the front passenger seat and then he put her suitcase between the seats behind her.

He concentrated on merging with the approaching traffic before he asked her, "Where are you headed?"

"Wichita", she replied.

Wichita, he thought. *I thought she was only going a few miles!*

He drove on a few minutes in silence. Then, almost as if the words sneaked out of his mouth unbidden, he said, "That's just where I'm going."

He knew he didn't have time to go to Wichita that morning. He had calls to make, a business to promote. But what would he do? Put her out on the side of the road and hope that someone else would pick her up?

I can't do that.

He kept driving past the intersection where he had originally planned to exit. He engaged the woman in conversation and learned that her husband had passed away more than six months ago. The old house where they had raised their children had not been properly cared for over the past several years and was, "falling down around our ears," she said. She had come to realize that she couldn't continue to live there alone and had shared that thought with her daughter. This daughter had recently moved to Wichita with her husband who had gotten a small promotion that had enabled them to buy a bigger house. She had invited her mother a few months ago to come live with her.

"So, she's expecting you?"

She was quiet for a few moments. "Well, I never told her I was coming, but I know it'll be alright."

He couldn't help wondering whether she hadn't called her daughter for fear she would tell her not to come.

He heard her stomach growling and figured that she had not eaten that morning. They were approaching a small town that boasted both a Braum's and a McDonalds. He asked her which she preferred, and she chose Braum's. They had breakfast and got back on the road.

When they got to Wichita, he had to stop at a convenience store to ask directions to the daughter's house. They had a street address and the old woman knew it was on the west side of town, but she had no idea how to get there. It turned out that the address was only a few miles away, and in a few minutes, he pulled up in from of a small, white frame house. The woman sat there for long moments, looking at the door. He got out, helped her out and picked up her suitcase. They started walking toward the house when the door opened. A young woman stepped out, saw her mother, and came running to hug her and kiss her face. They were still standing together like that when he went back to his car and started off. He looked back to see the old woman wave at him. He waved back and smiled to himself.

Yes, he had to stop at a convenience store-gas station to get a car freshener. He thought she probably had not had an opportunity to bathe for a few days. So maybe she didn't smell like a prairie rose. Maybe he was going to be five hours or so behind the schedule he had set for himself, but he whistled happily to himself all the way home.

I don't even want to report this, but the fact is she was black and our salesman was white.

What difference does that make, you ask? None at all.

These were the kind of acts that Alexis de Tocqueville saw in America. This is what America is all about—what we were, what we have been, and hopefully what we always will be; a collection of good people concerned about each other.

Is that "goodness" still alive in America?

If not, can it be restored?

Should goodness be a part of the American culture?

Chapter 8

THE FRENCH REVOLUTION

HOW DIFFERENT THE French Revolution was from the revolution where America won its independence from England! Indeed, the Revolutionary War in the United States set off a chain of events that culminated in the creation of a constitution that guaranteed freedoms at which the rest of the world could only marvel.

In America, our war was with a foreign country; at least, a country across an ocean from us. We desired freedom to govern ourselves, develop our own systems for jurisprudence, schools, governance and protection from other states/countries.

France's war was for the purpose of wresting power from the hands of the aristocrats and clergy. It developed into a ghastly, blood-thirsty orgy of violence in which the guillotine was used to sever the heads of thousands of French citizens. For many, their only crime was that they were or had been wealthy. At least 40,000 people were killed via the guillotine. As many as 300,000 Frenchmen and women (1 in 50) were arrested during a ten-month period between September 1793 and July 1794. Included in these numbers were, of course, the deaths of Louis XVI and Marie Antoinette. Although all social classes and professions suffered, the death toll was especially high for both clergy and aristocrats. The numbers of those killed and taken into custody were probably even higher than these numbers reflect, as the documented numbers don't include people killed by vigilantes and other self-proclaimed representatives of the First French Republic.

Now do you understand better why Englishman Edmond Burke wrote as he did about the revolution in France? It was a black time in Europe. It was easy to conclude that chivalry was indeed dead on that continent. Lights had gone out—in the City of Lights—Paris.

In *Reflections on the Revolution in France*, Edmond Burke wrote:

> But the age of chivalry is gone. That of sophisters, economists, and calculators has succeeded, and the glory of Europe (and perhaps the world) is extinguished forever. Never, never more shall we behold that generous loyalty to rank and sex, that proud submission, that dignified obedience, that subordination of the heart, which kept alive, even in servitude itself, the spirit of an exalted freedom. The unbought grace of life, the cheap defence of nations, the nurse of manly sentiment and heroic enterprise, is gone! It is gone, that sensibility of principle, that chastity of honor, which felt a stain like a wound, which inspired courage whilst it mitigated ferocity, which ennobled whatever it touched, and under which vice itself lost half its evil, by losing all its grossness.

Because of the wanton murders in France that bore testimony to the brutality of their revolution, it is small wonder that Alexis de Tocqueville found in America what differences existed between the peoples of each country that contributed to the obvious success that America experienced after their War of Independence from Britain, in direct contrast with the French.

What the Frenchman found, and what underlay the American experiment with a democratic republic, was an attitude that is perhaps summed up best in this prayer that U.S. Senate Chaplain Peter Marshall offered many years ago:

> Lord Jesus, thou who art the way, the truth and the life; hear us as we pray for the truth that shall make us free. Teach us that liberty is not only to be loved but also to be lived. Liberty is too precious a thing to be buried in books. Help us to see that our liberty is not the right to do as we please, but the opportunity to please to do what is right.

Please to do, want to do, earnestly desire to do that which is right. That is America. When a majority of our citizens are striving to do the right thing, their influence reaches the rest of the country so that it is deemed unseemly to do anything that is egregiously wrong.

That is the *good* about America that Tocqueville wrote of; that which seeks what is in the best interests of others, rather than of the self.

Chapter 9

HOW DID WE GET TO BE SO DIVIDED?

Early Constitutional Challenges

COME TO THINK of it, it has been a bumpy road for the United States since the very beginning. Many Americans opposed Secretary of the Treasury Alexander Hamilton's creation of a national bank. They viewed that bank as a threat to states' rights, something that smaller states, particularly, saw as an infringement upon their prerogatives. When Hamilton used that new bank for the assumption of debt owed by states via bonds and scrip that they had issued (the Funding Act of 1790), the Washington administration pursued the policy, under Secretary Hamilton's leadership, to assume the outstanding debt of states that had not yet repaid their American Revolutionary War debts. A few states, among them the largest of the colonies, Virginia, had already repaid their debt, and thought that the program to help the smaller states was egregiously unfair. Hamilton not only stuck by his guns, but helped push through federal taxes to provide the money for repayment. There was a tariff imposed and an excise tax enacted on whiskey. The latter move actually set off a rebellion—The Whiskey Rebellion—by western farmers in protest. Indeed, the rebellion had to be put down by the United States military under the leadership of General (President) George Washington; one of the few times soldiers have been asked to fire on fellow citizens. The tax stuck, although most of the violators were pardoned, and the federal government thereby established its supremacy.

So, it is not as though the Constitution has gone unchallenged until recently. It has been challenged since its inception by a great number of people, with good motives and bad.

On the topic of secession, or withdrawing from the Union, James Madison wrote:

> "A Union of the States containing such an ingredient (to not allow any state to secede from the Union) seemed to provide for its own destruction. The use of force against a State would look more like a declaration of war, than an infliction of punishment, and would probably be considered by the party attacked as a dissolution of all previous compacts by which it might be bound."

After the dispute that prompted Madison to opine on secession, there was a later challenge to the authority of the federal government. South Carolina asserted its right to "nullify" any law by the federal government that it perceived to work a hardship on its citizens.

Nullification was controversial because it asserted the states' power over the federal government. Thomas Jefferson and James Madison had first conceived of the idea of nullification in their Kentucky and Virginia Resolutions, written secretly in 1798. The resolutions were written in response to the passage of the Alien and Sedition Acts of that same year. In essence, the resolutions stated that the federal government was a compact among the states, thus the states had the final say on what laws were unconstitutional and could then nullify them. This, however, was not the major controversy of nullification. That would come in the late 1820s and early 1830s when South Carolina would attempt to nullify the Tariff of 1828 and declared its right to secede from the union.

President Andrew Jackson declared the proposed nullification of this tariff to be a treasonous act, and he sent warships off the coast of South Carolina until that state agreed to follow the provisions of the tariff of 1828.

Not every attempt of the United States to "purify" itself and rein in the more egregious nasty habits was met with success.

In the United States, Prohibition was a nationwide constitutional ban on the sale, production, importation, and transportation of alcoholic beverages that remained in place from 1920 to 1933.

The people of the U.S. protested from the very beginning. There were "speakeasy" bars on almost every corner in the larger cities. These places, also called "blind pig" or "blind tiger," were bars where a person could buy an illegal drink of liquor in the days of the Prohibition era. Many believed that the change in the Constitution which had established Prohibition and made it illegal to manufacture, transport or sell alcohol was an answer to a serious crime problem. Prohibition was introduced as the 18th Amendment to the United States Constitution in January of 1919. Drinking alcohol was viewed by some as a violation of God's law. Others thought most crime was tied in one way or another to the exorbitant use of alcoholic drinks. People did not openly flaunt the law, but everybody knew these places existed and the law did little or nothing about them.

Unfortunately, there were never enough agents, so-called *revenuers,* to police the illegal production and distribution of alcohol. The agents received low pay, were not well-trained, received very little moral support, and very shortly after the 18th Amendment was enacted, public sentiment, which had been in favor of Prohibition, turned against it, and so Prohibition was abolished by the 21st

Amendment. Citizens saw that the result of Prohibition was to drive the sale and consumption of alcohol underground and create an underworld of lawbreakers, such as Al Capone, who fought over the tremendous profits from illegal whiskey.

A bill to repeal Prohibition was passed on February 20, 1933. The 36th state, Utah, ratified the amendment on December 5, 1933, and it became the law of the land. Chalk up a victory for those who rejected any sort of interference with their right to decide for themselves what was good and what was evil. From the nation's beginning, there have been many such challenges of the law and how to enforce it, but the Constitution has been durable and flexible enough to provide opportunities for a solution to those challenges.

SECTION II

Wars Reveal
A Nation's Character

Chapter 10

WORLD WARS I AND II

This is a war to end all wars.
-American President Woodrow Wilson

Only the dead have seen the end of war.
-George Santayana, Spanish-American philosopher,
in a counter to Wilson's words

IT SEEMS A disservice to devote only a single chapter to events as important as the First and Second World Wars. These wars changed the face of the globe, and in one or two instances, set in motion grievances which played an important role in future conflicts. However, war is not the focus of this book. Rather, the only purpose in mentioning these two conflicts is to dramatize the differences in which wars are fought today.

WWI was begun not because Archduke Ferdinand of Austria was assassinated, although our history books list that as the major cause. No, the real reason(s) for the war had more to do with lands being held by people who spoke the language of an adjoining country and wished to be reunited with their fellows, or the desire of Russia to invade the Ottoman Empire so that they could establish consuls in ports with access to all seas formerly somewhat closed to them. They had no year-round seaport. Icy conditions closed their northern ports at times in winter. Unfortunately for the Russians, while much of their army was away fighting the Ottoman Empire, a revolution (The Bolshevik Revolution) broke out in the homeland. It succeeded, at least in part, because of the absence of troops loyal to the royal family in and around Moscow. The vicissitudes of war!

Much like the struggle between India and Pakistan for the various provinces of Kashmir, the Kurds have for centuries been under the hegemony of other states. Their aspirations received a setback when, after WWI, lands wherein the Kurds resided were divided between Turkey and Iraq. There is still no land for the Kurds as neither of those countries has been willing to relinquish any of their land for the formation of an independent Kurdistan.

Much of the old Ottoman Empire was partitioned between England, France, Italy and Russia.

The important thing for our purposes is that there were winners and losers in WWI, with Germany being the biggest loser. In fact, a land-grab of three German provinces by the French—Alsace, Lorraine and the Saar—while Belgium got part of another German province, and a later invasion by French and Belgian troops that took the Ruhr Province from Germany (ostensibly to make it impossible for Germany ever again to have a dominant army) almost guaranteed that there would be a second world war. The Saar was a highly industrialized area of western Germany, and the Ruhr had great deposits of coal and iron ore. Absent those steps that exceeded the terms of the Treaty of Versailles, a second world war might have been avoided, because the treaty was meant to illustrate the futility and the cost of war so that wiser men might avoid it at all costs. The excuse that France and Belgium provided for their invasion of the Ruhr was non-payment of fines that the Treaty of Versailles had levied against Germany after the war. The fact is that Germany, experiencing runaway inflation, could not carry out the functions of government, let alone repay onerous debt.

The invasion of the Ruhr by France and Belgium in 1923 so angered the German people that they became much more amenable to and accepting of the promises that communists and the National Socialist Party made to restore the grandeur that Germany had once enjoyed.

After several pitched battles in the streets of Germany, Adolph Hitler's National Socialist Party edged out the communists, and while they never won an election outright, Nazis eventually replaced the Weimar Republic that had been promulgated by the Versailles Treaty. By the mid-twenties, and in violation of the Versailles accords, the Germans were secretly manufacturing weapons, ships and airplanes.

In 1938, British Statesman Neville Chamberlain met with Adolph Hitler at Berchtesgaden in Germany to seek a peaceful accord and avert war. He returned to England, telling the British that he believed that he had, "secured peace for our time." All it had cost was ceding a part of Czechoslovakia (known as the Sudetenland) to Germany, and the Germans promised that they would not make war on anyone else.

It was only months after occupying Sudetenland that Germany began invading other countries, including Poland, France, Belgium and Austria. The United States, despite heavy pressure from Britain, France and others, refused to involve herself in the war—until the Japanese attacked a U.S. Base in Hawaii called Pearl Harbor on December 7, 1941. We quickly found ourselves involved in a two-front war—a European and a Pacific theater.

Once again, the Allies, of which the United States was a principal member, prevailed. Both the Germans and the Japanese were forced to sign what were known as unconditional surrenders, admitting fault and acknowledging defeat. Unlike the treaty with which WWI was ended, there were no real punitive measures taken against Japan or Germany. To be sure, limitations were placed on the size and scope of their armed forces, and both lands were occupied by small contingents of the armies of the victors. Indeed, America helped both Japan and Germany recover economically from that devastating war—a drastic change from the Treaty of Versailles.

A mistake? Not from a general sense. It seemed a good idea in terms of trade and economic assistance. But should there have been more punitive actions taken to discourage future wars?

Most historians agree that the terms offered the losers in WWII were generous, and for the most part, correct.

Chapter 11

BRIEF PEACEFUL INTERLUDE

I THOUGHT I HAD read—even experienced—a time of peace and relief after the conclusion of WWII. Perhaps I was wrong. I can find no record of peaceful feelings experienced anywhere in America after that horrendous war.

From the mid-'30s until after the conclusion of the Second World War in 1945, America was pre-occupied with the Great Depression and the growing threat of war. Efforts were being made by combatants on both sides to persuade America to join the conflict. We were, of course, late getting into the conflict, only responding when the Japanese bombed our military facilities at Pearl Harbor on the island of Oahu, Hawaii. It was still a long and bitter struggle, costing America many billions of dollars and the lives of many U.S. military personnel—*what has been justly called America's greatest generation.*

The Allies, of which we were a part, won World War II when first the Germans and then the Japanese signed surrender documents. It should be noted that these documents iterated the fact that these two countries, Germany and Japan, sued the Allies for peace and thereby ceded defeat. We won. They lost. Period.

America's returning soldiers were only interested in re-establishing their lives, catching up on the lost years and trying to discover what a normal life was like. Things were quiet for a few years. The late '40s and beginning of the '50s were comfortable years in

America for the most part. There was a popular magazine called *The Saturday Evening Post*. That magazine featured an artist named Norman Rockwell who drew every cover for the *Post* for years. His drawings were often humorous, sometimes poignant, but they inevitably illustrated Main Street America. It was like holding a mirror up so that the nation could see itself—and like what it saw. America felt good about herself.

Chapter 12

THE KOREAN POLICE ACTION

Often referred to as "The Forgotten War"

THEN BEGAN THE Korean Police Action, as it was called; a United Nations effort—several nations sent troops to fight against the aggressor, North Korea, whose army was trained by the Soviet Union. The conflict began on June 25, 1950, when 75,000 North Koreans crossed the border at the 38th Parallel which separates North Korea from South Korea. The North was provided arms and other war materiel by China. The South was backed by the United Nations, mostly American troops, that entered the action in July of 1950—less than a month after the start of hostilities. This long, bloody and often freezing conflict lasted until an armistice was signed in July of 1953—after the loss of some five million soldiers and civilians. *It is significant that this was the first war that the United States did not outright win.* Indeed, that armistice signed in 1953 is still in effect; there has never been a peace treaty signed to end the war.

We should never minimize the tremendous costs of the Korean War. Men who had already fought one world war were pressed back into duty to face the Korean hordes that poured over the 38th Parallel. It was brutal fighting in a most harsh and inhospitable land.

When the United States initially entered the conflict under the brilliant leadership of General Douglas MacArthur, the Americans and their United Nations allies quickly pushed the North Koreans back, winning battle after battle. MacArthur sought and gained permission from President Harry Truman to push on into North Korea and finish the war. To obtain this permission, MacArthur had assured the President that he did not think the Communist Chinese would get involved on the side of the North Koreans.

He was very much mistaken. Allied troops were well into the North when hordes of Chinese soldiers swarmed over the Yalu River, the boundary between North Korea and China, to the Korean front, overwhelming the allied army with vastly superior numbers.

General MacArthur, having miscalculated China's response, then informed the President he believed that America should retaliate against China by sending bombers into China, destroying ammunition and military supplies and Chinese and North Korean railroads and highways. If this sounds rather ambitious, you should perhaps be reminded that at a November 1950 press conference, President Truman had told reporters he *would take whatever steps were necessary to win in Korea, including the use of nuclear weapons. Those weapons, he added, would be controlled by military commanders in the field.*

In April of the following year, Truman put the finishing touches on what was to be a plan for nuclear war in Korea. He allowed nine nuclear bombs with fissile cores to be transferred into Air Force custody and transported to Okinawa. Truman also authorized another deployment of atomic-capable B-29s to Okinawa. Strategic Air Command set up a command-and-control team in Tokyo.

At that November press conference, Truman had told reporters those nuclear weapons would be controlled by military commanders in the field. (That would be... General MacArthur!)

Did President Truman lie? Or did circumstances on the ground force him to reconsider his authorization of the use of nuclear weapons?

MacArthur had assured Truman the Chinese would not invade into North Korea, and further predicted that the Soviets would not allow themselves to be drawn into the conflict. Having seen that the General erred in his initial estimate, Truman balked at widening the scope of the war. An angry MacArthur took his dispute with the President public with a letter to House Republican Leader Joseph Martin.

In his *The General vs. the President: MacArthur and Truman at the Brink of Nuclear War,* the historian H. W. Brands wrote:

> MacArthur thought that if we go to war, we go to war. Any commander in battle wants to protect those forces, and to send men into battle knowing he can't use all potential resources is exceedingly frustrating. That's going to get any general upset... *World War II, however, was the last war that Americans have been able to fight **all out**.* [writer's emphasis] The reason, we are informed, is that the dangers of escalation outweigh the benefits of victory.

One would be on solid ground to ask for whom would the dangers be too great? To our armies, or to the politicians desiring to be re-elected?

MacArthur's strategy was sound, but President Truman believed such an aggressive move might bring not only China, but the Soviet Union into the fray—making it what it had been all along, a war between democracy and communism. Indeed, Soviet Premier Josef Stalin told Mao Zedong of China that he would not authorize Soviet fighters over North Korea but he would protect Chinese supply routes in China. Even that protection would be three weeks in coming (which would have made it too late to help the Chinese if Truman had signed off on the plan to use nuclear weapons), but perhaps Truman didn't know that. In any event, General MacArthur was adamant to the point that Truman fired him—possibly the most popular and respected general in U.S. history—and replaced him with General Matthew Ridgeway.

Who was right, Truman or MacArthur?

Were Truman and the leading politicians at the time thinking truly about what was best for America, or were the politicians, particularly, more concerned with winning the next election?

Most historians side with Truman. However, had the U.S. continued into China, destroyed the lines of resupply and eradicated their vast stockpiles of guns and ammunition, the war might have been won—and over in a short time.

That's only conjecture, but we must recognize that this is the first time America had accepted something other than complete victory in war. Is that important? For one thing, that "settling for a tie" sent a message to the entire world, particularly our enemies, who might now be tempted to challenge America to a war if they could be reasonably assured America no longer fought wars in order to win them. America *did* eventually end hostilities with a negotiated cease-fire and truce. The lines separating North from South Korea remained the 38th Parallel, all Chinese and allied troops ceased hostilities, and that temporary truce remains in effect today. It was a bitter pill for many Americans to swallow, not following MacArthur's direction and driving the Chinese out of North Korea, thus winning the war. *Perhaps that was a significant turning point in American history—when we first settled for a draw rather than victory.*

The Chinese called our bluff—and we blinked.

One of the principal things that a person, group or nation must possess before it can win any sort of contest—a game, a fight, a promotion... or a war... is *desire*, the will to win. If that desire to win—if the grievance over which the war is precipitated is insufficient to warrant an all-out effort—then don't even *think* about declaring hostilities! There is an ancient admonition to be slow to enter a fight. However, once you are drawn into a conflict the focus shifts. You must now concentrate upon doing whatever it takes to come out of that contest a winner. Wars with some foes are so bitter that the only alternative to winning is *abject surrender*, perhaps even the death of many or most of the civilian population of the losing side.

I admit that we now live in a world where there is sometimes little distinction drawn between winners and losers. Both individuals and teams engaged in a sporting contest receive a trophy, often of a similar size and grandeur. In some games among our young, officials don't even keep score.

I recall the wonderful-sounding observation of Grantland Rice, a very famous sportswriter in the 1920s through the 1940s—"It is not whether you win or lose, but how you play the game." Of course, his point was to emphasize the importance of sportsmanship; an admirable thing. He was *not* recommending that we give no effort to win a game (or win a war to preserve our lives).

Tell a thug who is coming at you full tilt, armed with a knife and intending to rip your guts out that you don't choose to fight him. He'll be pleased to hear it. Will he stop in his pursuit to do you harm? He will not. If you fail to defend yourself, all you will have done is make the attacker's job far easier.

Victory in military conflict is obtained by inflicting more losses upon the enemy, in land and holdings but particularly in manpower, than the enemy can sustain. When their losses become unbearable, the enemy will sue for peace—on the victor's terms. That is a victory. A negotiated truce or peace may well be construed as a win, perhaps even for both sides. But it is *not* a victory for either side. Why is that an important concept to keep in mind? Because someone who has been thoroughly defeated—maybe humiliated—will not soon forget the shellacking it was forced to endure, nor be anxious for a second round of battles.

Just one good example should suffice to illustrate the point. The tiny nation of Japan defeated the much larger Russia in a war that began in 1904. Japan conquered the peninsula of Korea and drove into Manchuria, the southwest part of which had been taken from China by the Russians. Japan quickly established mastery of the nearby seas, and although the Russians had completed the Trans-Siberian Railroad all the way from Moscow into Vladivostok on their extreme east coast, they were unable to keep their army fully supplied with manpower and munitions. That fact, plus poor leadership on the part of the Russian officer corps, made Japan the victor. While Japan was allowed to keep much of the territory it had conquered, Russia had to cede Manchuria back to the Chinese. Russia has been reluctant to quarrel with the Japanese since that disastrous defeat. Once burned, twice shy, as the saying goes.

So wars—particularly those that are decisively won and lost—have a lasting effect on the participants—winners and losers.

Do nations have the same deep recollection of those wars or *police actions* which drag on for years and then end in a non-decision? Those conflicts often leave a bitter taste in the mouths of the combatants on either side; not necessarily fear or dread of the former enemy. A famous college football coach, Paul 'Bear' Bryant, when asked by a sportswriter whether a tie was as good as a win, said, "Hell, no! A tie is like kissing your sister." Allowing a protracted war to end in an armistice rather than a suit for peace on the part of the loser may be markedly worse than kissing your sister.

One other factor of some importance in the Korean conflict may have been that President Truman and powerful senators were more risk-averse than was General MacArthur. Then again, just as Adolph Hitler's insane jealousy of General Erwin Rommel led directly to his (Hitler's) making poor decisions as to how the Nazis could best prosecute the war, there might have been a little jealousy on the part of Truman regarding the vast popularity of MacArthur, whose exploits in the Pacific theater were the stuff of legend. Hitler's envy might have cost Germany a victory, and a similar set of circumstances might have existed in Korea.

One thing most historians might agree upon is that had MacArthur been allowed to decimate the armies of China and its war machinery in 1951, the later costly war that spread from Vietnam to Cambodia and Laos might well have been forestalled. Would China have become the military powerhouse it is today? Highly unlikely. A question remains: *could* MacArthur have defeated the Chinese? Or, as President Truman and many others feared would be necessary, could America have defeated the combined forces of China and the Soviet Union? The North Korean Army (NRK) fought battles as the Soviets had taught them—and quite differently from the way the Chinese, not nearly as well equipped, prosecuted war.

America had driven the North Korean forces out of their own country. Although much of it was grossly misinterpreted or misreported, all the intelligence the Americans had did support a supposition that should American troops drive north of the Yalu River into China, it would *possibly* precipitate a Third World War with the Soviet Union, China and North Korea as adversaries. With these three countries on one side and the allied forces, principally America, on the other, had America acted decisively we might well have won that war.

In Truman's defense, it had not been long enough since the Second World War for the American people to have time to forget the terrible costs, deprivation and loss of loved ones. They had no appetite for widening the current conflict. Also, according to testimony given after Truman had fired General MacArthur, U.S. military intelligence disclosed that it believed that there were "around 85" Soviet submarines in the waters off Korea (probably an exaggeration). Their presence brought up the fear of an alliance between the Russian Bear and the Chinese hordes to form a formidable force that the President thought might overwhelm the United Nations armies in North Korea. Just in sheer numbers, those two nations, the Soviet Union and China, could have put two to three times as many soldiers in the field as the United States. Our intelligence feared those two might not only drive us from Korea, but continue on to capture Vietnam, Cambodia, Laos and even Malaysia. (Almost all those defeats did eventuate, years later). Truman, with the full support of the Joint Chiefs of Staff, blinked. Who is to say that it was the wrong decision? Could America, under the leadership of General MacArthur, have won a war with China at that time? There is now no way to know that. *One thing is certain, however—you cannot win a contest in which you decline to participate.*

Did we learn anything from the Korean Police Action?

> "What experience and history teaches us is that people and governments have never learned anything from history, or acted on principles deduced from it."
> — **Georg Wilhelm Friedrich Hegel**, Allen W. Wood (editor), Raymond Guess, (Editor). Published by Cambridge University Press-1991.

Do so-called "civilized" nations have a strong tendency to hang on tightly to the wealth and its accoutrements they have accumulated rather than risk it in a fight for the preservation of liberties and freedoms for other nations—and even for themselves? The more you have to lose, the more reluctant you become to put it all on the line, even in defense of your own liberties—and this is unfortunate in many respects.

Another factor that should be introduced here is the possibility that if a hard life produces hard people, which history shows is at least somewhat true, then perhaps the reverse is true—an easy life produces a citizenry that is not so eager for physical exertion, or more importantly for our discussion, confrontation. They begin to enjoy the fact that they do not have to work as hard as their fathers. If they work at all, their job is unlikely to involve hauling bales of hay from the field to the barn in 100-degree heat for their entire summer "vacation."

Even if that theory should be true—that an easy life produces softer people—that is not a bad thing in and of itself. One would hope that with a more stable life and a wealthier, more educated populace life should be easier—for all people. But history shows it doesn't work out that way. Citizens with a lot of time on their hands and nothing important to do seem to get into much more mischief and accomplish far less of a positive nature than do those who work hard all day at a demanding job. Funny how that seems to be true.

Affluence—not really a terrible word—has been associated with some behaviors not in the least laudable. Ethan Couch from Burleson, Texas made national headlines in 2013 when four people were killed in the crash of a car Ethan was driving. His lawyers used the "affluenza" defense, saying the Couch family's wealth prevented their son from having an understanding of the consequences of his actions. Although he was found guilty, he got off with probation, largely because of that defense.

Children in America today may be the most coddled of any generation, and perhaps more than any nation in man's history. Such tame play as tag, kickball, dodge ball, playing on glider swings, etc.—these have all been deemed unsafe for today's elementary-age children. It is far safer to play video games all day. Certainly, you are not likely to be physically harmed—unless it is a strained thumb from moving all of those keys so rapidly on a GameBoy.

I wish that this was a rhetorical question; it is not.

If the United States were to be invaded by (you name it—Russia, China), would America's youth respond by joining a branch of the Armed Forces in sufficient numbers to repel the invaders? Do they really know how to fight, and are freedom and liberty still that important to us?

Chapter 13

VIETNAM WAR

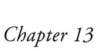

American soldiers returning home from Vietnam often faced
scorn as the war they had fought in became increasingly unpopular.
-**_Dante A. Ciampaglia_**-*History; updated 3/19/2019*

IN SPITE OF the interruption of the Korean War, America had gone back to a relatively peaceful way of living after WWII. For the most part, schools in our country were good to excellent. Churches were often full to overflowing on a given Sunday. Happiness, laughter and a feeling of prevailing peace abounded in the United States. It was also reflected in music heard on the radio and in the movies shown in theaters.

But something occurred in the early 1960s that in retrospect must be seen as a cataclysmic event. That was when America got involved in a conflict in another far-off East Asia country called Vietnam. The French had attempted to help South Vietnam defend itself from its aggressive communist northern neighbor. (Sound familiar?) They fought there from 1950, until a French fortress at a place called Dien Bien Phu fell to the North Vietnamese in May of 1954. In a peace accord signed by the French, Vietnamese and others, the countries of North and South Vietnam were separated at the 17th Parallel. All French troops were removed from Vietnam.

An uneasy peace held for a while, but the North Vietnamese continually violated the terms of the treaty so the United States began sending in "advisers" and "support personnel" to aid the South Vietnamese, as they had formerly helped the French. Before the war officially began for the U.S., our nation had more than 23,000 such people in Vietnam—possibly many more than that number. Dwight D. Eisenhower, President of the United States from 1953 until 1961, had sent military aid to the French troops in Vietnam, and when they withdrew from the South, he continued to send aid to the anti-communist leader of South Vietnam, Ngo Dinh Diem.

When Ho Chi Minh, the leader of North Vietnam, pushed his armies across the border separating the two states in March of 1959, the war took on a different aspect. There was a strong impetus in the United States to stay out of the actual fighting, but it was becoming increasingly clear that the South Vietnamese could not handle the armies of the North alone.

President John F. Kennedy assumed the office of the Presidency in 1961, and his administration realized almost immediately that a change must be made. The South Vietnamese could not sustain themselves without more than just advice and war materiel. They needed American troops to fight alongside them. In addition to other problems, Ngo Dinh Diem, the leader of the South Vietnam Government, stirred up anti-war sentiment in both his own country and in America. Officially, Diem was killed by a group of rebel generals three weeks prior to the death of President Kennedy in Dallas in November of 1963. It is believed by many that the Kennedy administration sanctioned the assassination (possibly by the CIA) because Diem was considered by many in the Kennedy administration to be a "loose cannon" that cost his country support from the U. S. Congress.

On March 8, 1965, with Lyndon Johnson now President, the first American combat troops landed just north of Da Nang, South Vietnam. This was the 3,500 troops of the 9th Marine Expeditionary Brigade, and the fighting began in earnest.

The Vietnamese War—or Conflict, rather—divided America as nothing had since the War Between the States—the so-called Civil War. *How can a war in which upwards of 600,000 soldiers, all citizens of the same nation, are killed, be called a "civil" war?*

There was a tremendous upheaval all across the United States in the '60s and early '70s. Many children, especially of the upper middle class and the wealthy, not only professed but offered proof that they rejected every tenet, every more, every custom—everything their parents held to be sacrosanct, their children rejected out of hand.

A focal point of this rebellion was the very unpopular war in Vietnam. This was something they used to unify their demonstrations; it was a ready catalyst. How diverse were these demonstrators and the agendas pushed by each? They ran the gamut from the Students for a Democratic Society (SDS), which sought anything *but* a democratic society. Then there were the Black Panthers who rejected the legitimacy of a white male-dominated government to rule them. There was also the Communist Party USA, headed by Gus Hall, an organization that funded these anti-government demonstrations and fanned the resentment and anger illustrated plainly at all such events. There was the Gay Liberation Front, now sub-divided into groups supporting all sexual acts once believed to be perverted or abnormal.

These demonstrations were always billed as "Peaceful Parades," non-violent exhibitions of the lack of trust the young people had in not just their government but of all American institutions. Of course, none of the demonstrations in San Francisco, where I served during that period with the FBI, were peaceful. The demonstrators brought their profanity-laced invective along with rocks, bricks—anything they could find to hurl at the police.

The primary demand of these demonstrators was that America pull out of Vietnam, regardless of the outcome. The Vietnam conflict was another war in which civilians were heavily involved in everyday decisions concerning the prosecution of the war. Men with absolutely no battlefield experience, who had never served a day in the military, were dictating to American generals how the war should be fought—what could and could not be done. They were the ones who set the *rules of engagement*. Politicians allowed the demonstrators to cow them into seeking peace at any price. Of course, liberal journalists had an immense amount of influence on them. In February 1968, in the wake of the Tet Offensive, the respected TV journalist Walter Cronkite, a liberal who had managed to present a moderate and somewhat balanced opinion regarding the war's progress, announced that it seemed "more certain than ever that the bloody experience of Vietnam is to end in a stalemate."

On the North Vietnamese side, they perceived correctly that the Tet offensive had been a failure. In battles in which they took the city of Hue from American and South Vietnamese soldiers only to lose it when the Americans counter-attacked, the North lost an estimated 5,000 soldiers killed, most of them hit by American air and artillery strikes. Although the Tet Offensive was *unsuccessful* from a military standpoint, it had an enormous impact.

Despite its heavy casualty toll and its failure to inspire widespread rebellion among the South Vietnamese, the Tet Offensive proved to be a strategic success for the North Vietnamese.

Before Tet, General William Westmoreland and other representatives of the Johnson administration had been claiming that the end of the war was in sight. But if the soldiers were to be bound by rules of engagement that literally made it impossible to win the war, it was now clear that a long struggle still lay ahead. Westmoreland requested more than 200,000 new troops in order to mount an effective counteroffensive, an escalation that many Americans saw as an act of desperation.

As a result, a "peace offensive", led by Dr. Henry Kissinger, began holding meetings with the North Vietnamese leader Le Duc Tho in Paris, France. America began the process of extracting our military from Vietnam. Our last soldiers were transported from the top of the U.S. Embassy building in Saigon, South Korea by helicopter—with Vietnamese civilians hanging on desperately to the skids.

It was a most ignominious retreat—not because the United States had been defeated by an enemy, but rather that the United States government, and perhaps the more vociferous American people, had lost the will to fight and had refused to provide the weapons and authority American soldiers needed to win the war.

In terms of the retreat, the British Expeditionary Force had been in a similar situation almost thirty years earlier; stranded with their back to the English Channel on the beaches of Dunkirk, France, during World War II. The German Army with tanks and armor was bearing down on them. The English people rallied in support of their forces and snatched victory from the very jaws of defeat, rescuing almost the entire British Expeditionary Force, returning them to England on any craft that could make the voyage across the channel, turning Dunkirk into a strategic victory in that they lived to fight again. And fight, they did! There were 338,000 soldiers evacuated from Dunkirk—including 100,000 French military personnel.

Well, Saigon was America's Dunkirk. We got most of our own forces out, but we left our allies, the Vietnamese people, to face the horrors of the North Vietnamese troops who were at the very gates. I will never forget the film footage of Vietnamese civilians clinging desperately to the skids of that last helicopter to fly off the embassy roof, some falling to almost certain death when they could hang on no longer.

The fault for that humiliating defeat cannot be laid at the feet of the brave soldiers who fought and sacrificed there. No, that dubious honor must be placed where it belongs—in the laps of America's politicians.

Just as an individual has a core of immutable beliefs, a character around which he/she builds their life that guides them in decision making—just so, a nation has a national character. There are certain things that a country cannot do and continue to call itself a nation of caring, loyal people, a people to whom integrity is an important part of their being. Abandoning allies is not a way to burnish that reputation.

Saigon is not a pleasant memory for Americans.

Another factor that brings back haunting memories is the shabby treatment the American troops got when they returned home. No troops who fought in any previous war were ever subjected to the disrespect, the shouted curses, being spat upon by crowds who should have received them as returning heroes. The soldiers had done an excellent job. Congress and the anti-war protest groups let them down.

You have heard the old maxim that when the going gets tough, the tough get going—and not for the exit. If you do not fully intend to win and to provide our military with all the weapons and war materiel to accomplish that victory, and unless you are going to allow them the freedom to fight without overly-restrictive "rules of engagement," then surrender—before you lose a single soldier.

SECTION III

Defining Morality Downward

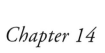

Chapter 14

THE FREE SPEECH MOVEMENT, OR 'JUSTIFICATION' FOR VULGARITY

The Rev. Jeremiah Wright, Jr. of Chicago's Trinity United Church of Christ, and Barack Obama's pastor since 1988, told his congregation in a sermon on Sept. 16, 2001, "The Day of Jerusalem's Fall," that U.S. terrorism had precipitated Al-Qaeda's attack. "We bombed Hiroshima, we bombed Nagasaki, and we nuked far more than the thousands in New York and the Pentagon, and we never batted an eye. We have supported state terrorism against the Palestinians and black South Africans, and now we are indignant because the stuff we have done overseas is now brought right back to our own front yards." Wright concluded with "America's chickens are coming home to roost." Daniel Pipes – Middle East Forum

THE LARGELY STUDENT-LED rebellion that began in the 1960s was not as much a coming-out party for young people who had discovered new truths by which to be guided as it was a rejection of all the old rules by which their parents had lived. There was no time to weigh and measure the outcomes of the destruction of "establishment" America. If what we as a nation were doing was not adopted within the past three years, it was no longer relevant. How, you may ask, does a group of people bent upon disobedience to law and any other type of limitations placed upon them, convince themselves that the solutions they propose (few, in the beginning) were superior to the practices that had been carried on since man came out of caves? It turned out to be no problem at all. You simply adopt the principle that nobody above the age of 30 is to be trusted, and the rest is easy.

How much hubris, arrogance, and superciliousness was required for these young rebels to assume that all the intelligence of the past centuries, all the ideas that governed society and the relations between individuals and nations that had been developed over the past thirty centuries or so had been absolutely wrongheaded?

If you were not alive and above the age of 30 when the Free Speech Movement had its genesis in, of all places, Berkeley, California on the campus of the University of California in 1964, you can only have a limited idea how painful it was to watch everything you had been taught was good and right denounced as wrong and deleterious to our nation. Had the protesters accepted that maybe a few of the practices of their elders were worthy of continuing into the future, their message would have been a little more palatable to the older generation. But no. There had never been a more complete rejection of the leadership of a nation, its customs and mores. How was it possible that our nation lasted as long as it had if all the principles upon which it was established were completely the reverse of reality?

It was like starting all over again—reinventing the wheel, so to speak—except that the likelihood that the new wheel would even be round was much in doubt if the leaders of the Students for a Democratic Society (SDS) or the Free Speech Movement of Mario Savio were involved in its design. This is not to disparage the intelligence of these individuals, but merely to point out the complete lack of experience any of them had with any form of leadership. The absence of a sound basis upon which to build a new workers' society did not seem to deter the rebellious masses, who aligned themselves with the Third World Liberation Front, the Communist Worker's Party, Students for a Democratic Society, the Berkeley Gay Liberation Front and any other group that opposed the war in Vietnam. How could so many ills be addressed and still retain a modicum of cohesion in these disparate movements? Some people within those groups had a good deal of talent in reaching a balance wherein all or most of the groups felt included in an exciting revolution.

The following is an excerpt from *the* speech made by Mario Savio on the steps of Sproul Hall on the Berkeley campus of the University of California:

> ... But we're a bunch of raw materials that don't mean to be—have any process upon us. Don't mean to be made into any product! Don't mean—Don't mean to end up being bought by some clients of the University, be they the government, be they industry, be they organized labor, be they anyone! We're human beings! ... There's a time when the operation of the machine becomes so odious— makes you so sick at heart—that you can't take part. You can't even passively take part. And you've got to put your bodies upon the gears and upon the wheels, upon the levers, upon all the apparatus, and you've got to make it stop. And you've got to indicate to the people who run it, to the people who own it, that unless you're free, the machine will be prevented from working at all.

This was heady stuff to teenagers, many of whom had never enjoyed real freedom from the restrictions placed upon them by their parents until arriving on the Berkeley campus.

Other campuses in California and across America were infected with the idea that the entire capitalist system was rigged against the young and the poor. One campus where the demonstrators succeeded for a time in literally shutting down the institution was the College of San Francisco, which later changed its name to the University of San Francisco.

There was a term widely used by the leadership of the student radicals in the '60s and '70s. It was *the military-industrial complex.* This reflected a belief that there was some sort of an illicit cabal connecting the political leaders, the industrial leaders, and those who headed up the military. The members of this cabal were alleged to be mean, wicked, and avaricious. Each existed for the other's benefit with little or no regard for what was good for the country or its people. The political leaders felt that they must project strength, which required a large standing military, which had to be supplied by those captains of industry. For those citizens who were enamored with the idea of redistributing the nation's wealth, the military-industrial complex made that virtually impossible by solidifying that wealth in the hands of the elite. While facts support the claim that the three major levels of wealth change very much, and very often, there is the impression that the rich continue to get richer and the poor continue to get poorer.

Would the ideas outlined above have been enough to radicalize the youth of America without the existence of the war in Vietnam alone? In all probability, no.

From Wikipedia's article about Samuel I. Hayakawa, a president of San Francisco State University:

> In 1968–69, there was a bitter student and Black Panthers strike at San Francisco State University in order to establish an ethnic studies program. It was a major news event at the time and chapter in

the radical history of the United States and the Bay Area. The strike was led by the Third World Liberation Front supported by Students for a Democratic Society, the Black Panthers and the countercultural community.

It proposed fifteen "non-negotiable demands," including a Black Studies department chaired by sociologist Nathan Hare independent of the university administration and open admission to all black students. The goal was to "put an end to racism," and the unconditional, immediate end to the War in Vietnam and the university's involvement in that conflict. It was threatened that if these demands were not immediately and completely satisfied the entire campus was to be forcibly shut down. Hayakawa became popular with conservative voters during this period after he pulled the wires out from the loudspeakers on a protester's van at an outdoor rally. Hayakawa relented on December 6, 1968 and created the first-in-the-nation College of Ethnic Studies.

The creation of that college with no applicable market for any degree obtained in that field of study may have been the beginning of the end for the American educational system. Instead of providing their students with a degree in a pursuit with which they could earn a living and contribute to the total growth of the economy, the leadership of colleges and universities all over the United States capitulated to the errant wishes of their students—to the detriment of all.

Hayakawa vehemently opposed the radical movement at first, winning conservative approbation. On one occasion, when a flat-bed truck was being used as a speaker's platform, complete with a microphone and speakers with which the student orators were demanding courses in Ethnic Studies, Black Studies, female and gay studies, Hayakawa hopped up on the trailer, wrested the microphone from the speaker and told his listeners that if they succeeded in forcing the university to adopt those courses, any degree they might obtain from that institution would "not be worth the paper it was written on." I was in the audience that day and agreed with Hayakawa's initial assessment—then and now.

Those born after the time when ethnic courses radically changed the college curriculum have no frame of reference to compare education BFSM (Before the Free Speech Movement) and PFSM (Post-Free Speech Movement). Real comparisons—apples to apples, oranges to oranges—are impossible to make. Although it had long been the practice to alter the graduation requirements for college athletes—that is, universities had created "easy A" courses for athletes who would not have been eligible to meet the scholastic requirements to play. Everybody knew about them, and I suppose nobody paid any particular attention to the eventual consequences of such a watering-down of education. Ah, but this was different. Seemingly overnight, it became possible in some universities to obtain a "legitimate" degree in such pursuits as Black Studies, Women's Studies, Sexual Orientation Studies. So in a way, what S. I. Hayakawa predicted has come true. A student might graduate from a university with a degree that has no application, no practical use. What could one do with any kind of "Studies" degree?

Even the shortcomings of the radical changes in university education outlined above were indeed only part of the problem. In order to encourage high numbers in enrollments, colleges lowered the requirements for entrance, inviting those who had no business pursuing a college degree to take classes and work on some degree program. Perhaps more serious, something that might be construed as little short of criminal action, was the practice of universities and the U. S. government to provide "Student Loans" to these pseudo-students. That meant that they "graduated" with a useless degree and perhaps more than $100,000 in student debt that they would never be able to repay in a hundred years. If they were fortunate enough to find any kind of a job, the chances are that job paid close to the minimum wage, making servicing a debt of any size virtually impossible. More and more people attend more and more expensive colleges and universities for less and less return on their investment.

A serious historian and author, Will Durant, with his wife, Ariel, wrote an eleven-volume history of the important eras of history. In a sequel to that history called *The Lessons of History*, first published in 1968, they said this:

> Intellect is a vital force in history but can be a dissolvement and destructive power. Out of every hundred new ideas, ninety-nine or more will probably be inferior to the traditional responses which they propose to replace. No one man, however brilliant and well-informed, can come in one lifetime to such fullness of understanding as to safely judge and dismiss the customs and institutions of his society, for these are the wisdom of generations and centuries of experiment in the laboratory of history. A youth (or a whole passel of youths) boiling with hormones will wonder why he should not give full freedom to his sexual desires; and if he is unchecked by custom, morals and laws, he may ruin his life before he matures sufficiently to understand that sex is a river of fire that must be banked and cooled by a hundred restraints if it is

not to consume in chaos both the individual and
the group.

So the conservative who resists change is as valuable
as the radical who proposes it—perhaps as much
more valuable as roots are more vital than grafts.
It is good that new ideas should be heard, for the
sake of the few that can be used; but it is also good
that new ideas should be compelled to go through
the mill of objection, opposition and contumely;
this is the trial heat which innovations must survive
before being allowed to enter the human race. It is
good that the old should resist the young, and that
the young should prod the old; out of this tension,
as out of the strife of the sexes and classes, comes
a creative tensile strength, a stimulated development, a secure and basic unity and movement of
the whole.

Perhaps the dissolution of all things American (as conceived by
the Founding Fathers) began much earlier than the sixties. If it did,
the movement to reject all the foundational truths upon which the
nation had been founded went into overdrive in that decade. One
could essentially say that many things believed to be good before
the 1960s became bad, and many more things deemed to be bad
prior to that decade were afterwards perceived to be good. Right
and wrong exchanged definitions.

The Free Speech Movement referenced earlier was not for the
purpose of obtaining the right to debate political ideas or principles.
It was principally to inform those of us from the old school that
when a young speaker felt like dropping the f-bomb, he would drop
it—regardless of the makeup of the speaker's audience. It would

appear that free speech applied only to them and those who were spouting ideas with which they agreed. Otherwise they would shut the speaker down.

What happened in the mid-to-late sixties that changed America entirely?

Of course, the war in Vietnam was a very big factor, but there was more to it than that. For reasons not evident to most, objections to the war morphed into hatred for the United States—its armies, its government—indeed, all the institutions of the nation were rejected, including—and later specifically—the church. Why? What was the genesis of these strong anti-establishment feelings?

Conspiracies are far fewer in number than most believe. It would be foolish to blame anti-Americanism on conspiratorial actions adopted by the Communist Party, the secular humanists, socialists or any combination of dissidents. The truth may be closer to the "outs" jealousy of those in politics or any other position of leadership who happened to be the "ins" at the time. Some people believe that no idea can be a good one unless *I* or *my group* came up with it. But let me suggest another concept that defies congruity and yet is a real possibility—one that helps to explain Hollywood's love affair with the political left.

Many of the '60s radicals were young people from wealthy families, families that they had somehow come to resent and desired to separate from. You might think it is admirable for youth to reject the trappings of wealth in favor of a simpler life, perhaps based on another parameter for measuring success. That might have been one motivating factor for these young people, but it doesn't come near explaining the necessity of rejecting all things for which their parents stood. Is everything my parents believed false or unworthy? Many radicals of that time would have answered that question in the affirmative. Who persuaded them to believe that?

For a part of the answer to that question, we must go back to the schools and universities from which these radicals had graduated, or at least where they had attended.

I have chosen to include the bulk of a Townhall.com piece entitled "We Have a Virtue Problem, America," published on August 12, 2019 by noted writer, speaker and Christian Apologetics advocate, Alex MacFarland:

> I well remember the New Age hokum passed off as learning as part of my 5th and 6th grade public education, yes, deep in Bible-belt North Carolina. One teacher repeatedly coached us to learn about ESP (extra-sensory perception), and our class of naive rural kids was told that we could create our own reality through "visualization." (Believe me, I was on board, but it didn't work for me, though. Try as I might, the Farah Fawcett poster in my room just never did turn into an actual human. Oh, well.)
>
> By the time I entered college (1982), my heroes were anti-establishment types like John Lennon and Jim Morrison. Morrison famously screamed, "You cannot petition God with prayer!" and would shout to concert audiences, "There are no rules! There are no laws! Grab your neighbor and love him!" Such cultural icons seemed to be the heroes of most of my instructors, too. Not only did I read what my undergrad professors recommended (Abbie Hoffman, Nietzsche, Sartre, Rand, etc.), I studied their positions and worldview.

Honestly desiring to "get" where influential thinkers were coming from, I spent months carefully slogging through Darwin's *On the Origin of Species*. It was enlightening, getting to the last paragraphs in which Darwin urged that his theory be thoroughly weighed out in the sphere of classroom debate. I was surprised, because (a) Evolution was certainly not offered in class as a "theory," but was repeatedly insisted upon as inarguable "fact." And (b), because honest debate and evaluation of both sides (of virtually any topic) were not allowed in my secular educational journey.

Today, the few intrepid students who venture to speak up for God and country are usually mocked by the professors. Over the past 20 years, hundreds of students have shared with me stories of classroom humiliation when they tried to speak of Jefferson's reference to a Creator, Franklin's prayers at the Constitutional convention, or even Dr. King's belief in God's Ten Commandments.

Balanced examination of many key issues (God's existence, the nature of ethics, the Christian foundations of Western civilization, or how the church birthed the civil rights movement) would never take place in most universities today. I have listened to many diatribes on how bad America is; I have almost never heard a public university professor accurately explain to students what America is.

We are endlessly told that mention of God or morality violates the First Amendment. This is patently false. How is it that 21ˢᵗ century secularists seem to know more about the application of the First Amendment...than the God-fearing men who wrote the First Amendment?

The framers of the Constitution certainly didn't think public mention of God, the Bible, or morals was unconstitutional. To the contrary, Hamilton, Madison, Washington, Jefferson, and the whole lot insisted that acquiescence before God was necessary in order to maintain a civil society.

Yet, secular organizations have spent decades working to squelch mention of God, the Ten Commandments, and morality in public. Collectively, they amount to a self-appointed "thought police," and have really robbed generations of citizens of knowledge of our rich Judeo-Christian foundations. Respect for human life is all but gone from our culture, because belief in God and truth are all but gone from our laws, classrooms, entertainment, media, and culture. And whom do we have to thank for this "scrubbing" away of God and elimination of our conscience? The ACLU, progressives, and a dozen other activist groups absent of any objective convictions.

Our condolences to the bereaved in Texas and Ohio. But to those who maliciously work to keep America "free" from mention of each one's accountability to

God, our Maker... know that it's your restrictions on the expression and practice of virtue that have brought us to this tragic place.

Walter E. Williams, a professor of economics at George Mason University, makes these observations about ethnic studies programs in his article, "Academic Stupidity and Brainwashing":

> There's another very dangerous bit of academic nonsense happening, this time at the K-12 level of education. One America News Network anchor interviewed Mary Clare Amselem, education specialist at the Heritage Foundation, about the California Department of Education's proposed ethnic studies curriculum. The proposed ethnic studies curriculum would teach children that capitalism and father figures are racist.

> The Ethnic Studies Model Curriculum also includes gross anti-Israel bias and teaches about a Palestinian-led anti-Israel initiative called Boycott, Divestment and Sanctions. The curriculum also has students study issues of police brutality and asks teachers to find incidents of bias by police in their own communities. According to an article by Shelby Talcott in The Stream, California's proposed curriculum called for students to study lawmakers such as Democratic Minnesota Rep. Ilhan Omar and Democratic Michigan Rep. Rashida Tlaib, both of whom have supported the BDS movement and have been accused of anti-Semitic rhetoric.

> The proposed ethnic studies proposal has been removed from the California Department of Education website. House Minority Leader Kevin McCarthy, R-Calif., said, "While I am relieved that California made the obvious decision to revisit this wholly misguided proposal, we need to know why and how a blatantly anti-Semitic, anti-Israel, factually inaccurate curriculum made its way through the ranks of California's Department of Education." He added, "This was not simply an oversight—the California Department of Education's attempt to institutionalize anti-Semitism is not only discriminatory and intolerant, it's dangerous."

> Brainwashing our youngsters is a serious matter. The people responsible for the California Department of Education's proposal ought to be summarily fired.

A recent article in the *Washington Times* newspaper reported that the ratio of Democrat to Republican instructors in colleges and universities is about 11½ Democrats to 1 Republican. The most liberal department in these colleges is—unsurprisingly—history.

The least liberal department? Economics. That also figures, if you think about it.

This compares to a 1968 study that reported the ratio of Democrat to Republican in our universities was 2.7 to 1. As recently as 2004, that ratio in various measures was seen as low as 9 to 1 all the way up to 15 to 1. So is it getting worse? It's hard to tell. One thing appears to be certain: with the increase in gender, sex and race-based studies, that ratio is not going to get better.

Kim R. Holmes, a distinguished fellow at The Heritage Foundation and the author of *The Closing of the Liberal Mind*, said the ascendance of multiculturalism in the humanities makes it difficult for conservatives to find work teaching.

If you're going to have a Gender Studies Department, or something like that, the progressive assumptions are built into the very idea of the department, so you're not going to hire any conservative professors. Because of this, the imbalance has proliferated.

The disparity is highest at the most prestigious universities, the study finds.

It is instructive to note that a pair of Big 10 schools, Penn State and Ohio State, have a ratio of Democrat to Republican professors of 6 to 1 and 3.2 to 1, respectively.

How about Princeton and Columbia? Both are at a ratio of 30 to 1, Democrats to Republicans. Do you suppose their students get a balanced education at these universities? Do they get to hear both sides of any issue?

The most balanced university in the nation, among those in the study, was Pepperdine with a ratio of 1.2 Democrats to 1 Republican.

Why the disparity? What has happened in America to cause such a shift in thinking and behavior? We've cited a few things earlier; the war in Vietnam, the breakdown of discipline in schools and in our society in general.

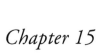

Chapter 15

USING TOLERANCE AS A CLUB

"Tolerance is the capacity to endure pain or hardship; sympathy or indulgence for beliefs or practices differing from or conflicting with one's own."—blog, 'Virtues for Life'

TOLERANCE—AN INNOCENT-SOUNDING WORD, seemingly benevolent in character, evocative of an adult attitude towards differences between individuals and cultures. That word has been used as a cudgel by the secular left for many years now and is presented to the "great unwashed"—that would be you and me—as the single-most important characteristic that an individual can develop; the posture of tolerance.

Presidential candidate Barack Obama spoke in 2008 about people in small-town Pennsylvania who had lost their jobs 25 years previously. He said, "And it's not surprising then they get bitter, they cling to guns or religion or antipathy toward people who aren't like them (like himself) or anti-immigrant sentiment or anti-trade sentiment as a way to explain their frustrations." That entire sentence, like many of the utterances of Barack Obama, makes no sense in the construction here that is taken from an issue of *Politico* magazine from April or May of 2008.

Those comments did not win him many friends in the Midwest and Southwest, but the point he was trying to make is that these people were incapable of understanding him and his message; primarily because he was different and bore none of their resentments.

I would invite you to ask yourself this question: who is the more intolerant—the people who cling to guns and/or religion, or those who use these allegations of intolerance as an explanation for the supposed prejudiced group's lack of support for someone who presents himself as one who is above that kind of bigotry?

Let's start with a definition from Merriam-Webster:

> tolerance
> noun
> tol·er·ance | \ 'tä-lə-rən(t)s , 'täl-rən(t)s\
> Definition of tolerance
> 1: capacity to endure pain or hardship: endurance, fortitude, stamina
> 2a: sympathy or indulgence for beliefs or practices differing from or conflicting with one's own
> 2b: the act of allowing something: TOLERATION.

It is impossible to have a full understanding of the real concept of tolerance unless you give proper emphasis to the first definition; the capacity to endure pain or hardship. That part of the definition seems to be of no consequence to the secularists who are demanding that the rest of us be more tolerant of their ideas. They are totally inconsiderate of how much pain the changes they demand of us causes. Their only concern is that all of us who disagree with them suffer in silence.

One of the things used to "sell" tolerance to the American people is the idea that being tolerant is "humane," the more "mature" behavior, the mode of conduct employed by all the more "intellectual" among us. Here's an example:

Someone or some group engages in bad behavior.

"We can tolerate this."

Something else deemed even more inappropriate comes up.

After a moments pause, we might grudgingly say, "We can tolerate that."

Another formerly taboo behavior is exhibited.

It only takes moments to conclude that, "This is only a little bit worse than what we have accepted before."

Are you familiar with the fable of the boiling frog?

The "Boiling Frog" is a fable describing a frog being slowly boiled alive. The premise is that if a frog is put suddenly into boiling water, it will immediately jump out. However, if the frog is put in tepid water which is then brought to a boil slowly, it will not perceive the danger and will be cooked to death.

The excuses for behavior that we are asked to overlook range from, "He had a deprived youth; one can't expect him to follow the rules perfectly," to, "He's intellectually challenged. Maybe he can learn later," or, "His parents have never explained that such behavior is wrong; it isn't his fault."

When acts that are "tolerable" are followed by acts a little less so and then those even more difficult to swallow, a person or nation can reach a point wherein it becomes **in**tolerable.

Is it possible that this kind of tolerance, a tolerance that feeds on itself, demanding more and more tolerance of more and more egregious conduct, led to the situation affecting many of our colleges and universities—even some of our larger cities?

While tolerance has been billed as one of the most admirable traits an individual might possess, is it possible that too much tolerance is a bad thing?

I love German Chocolate cake. Mmm-mmm. But somehow I understand that if I ate German Chocolate cake morning, noon and night, even though I washed it down with a healthy glass of milk at each meal, that cake diet would not result in optimal health. My body would be unable to tolerate that much sugar.

Just so, we need to understand that we have tolerated certain aberrant behaviors far beyond the point at which they have become detrimental to our national health. There are, indeed, certain acts and actions for which we have developed a tolerance that can lead to the destruction of our society and our nation. So no, tolerance is not always a good thing.

In his book entitled <u>Life at the Bottom,</u> in a chapter he called, "Seeing is not Believing," Theodore Dalrymple wrote, "Violence, vulgarity and educational failure: three aspects of modern English life that are so obvious and evident that it requires little observational power to discern them. Indeed, it requires far more mental effort and agility not to discern them, to screen them out of one's consciousness..."

From <u>Life at the Bottom</u> *by Theodore Dalrymple. Published in Great Britain by Ivan R. Dee, 2001.*

Dalrymple was writing about what he called the British "underclass," made up mostly of whites—and not necessarily the poorest of them. They appear to be a class unto themselves and appear to reject the rules and mores by which society from the Middle Ages forward has ruled itself. Thomas Sowell, American professor, author and lecturer, likens the British *underclass* to the American black *underclass.* Both writers decry the response of the intelligentsia of both nations to the problems posed by the underclass on both sides of the ocean. It is almost as though they deliberately turn a blind eye to the destruction; indeed, at times they, the intelligentsia, seem to be aiding and abetting their lawlessness.

Diversity Rules!

According to Minding the Campus, Penn State University's Office of Vice Provost for Educational Equity employs 66 staff members. The University of Michigan currently employs a diversity staff of 93 full-time diversity administrators, officers, directors, vice provosts, deans, consultants, specialists, investigators, managers, executive assistants, administrative assistants, analysts and coordinators. Amherst College, with a student body of 1,800 students employs 19 diversity people. Top college diversity bureaucrats earn salaries in six figures, in some cases approaching $500,000 per year. In the case of the University of Michigan, a quarter (26) of their diversity officers earn annual salaries of more than $100,000. If you add generous fringe benefits and other expenses, you could easily be talking about $13 million a year in diversity costs. The Economist reports that University of California, Berkeley, has 175 diversity bureaucrats.

Diversity officials are a growing part of a college bureaucracy structure that outnumbers faculty by 2 to 2.5 depending on the college. According to "The Campus Diversity Swarm," an article from Mark Pulliam, a contributing editor at Law and Liberty, which appeared in the City Journal (10/10/2018), diversity people assist in the cultivation of imaginary grievances of an ever-growing number of "oppressed" groups. Pulliam writes: "The mission of campus diversity officers is self-perpetuating.

Affirmative action (i.e., racial and ethnic preferences in admissions) leads to grievance studies.
Increased recognition of LGBTQ rights requires
ever-greater accommodation by the rest of the student body. Protecting 'vulnerable' groups from
'hate speech' and 'microaggressions' requires speech
codes and bias-response teams (staffed by diversocrats). Complaints must be investigated and
adjudicated (by diversocrats). Fighting 'toxic masculinity' and combating an imaginary epidemic of
campus sexual assault necessitate consent protocols,
training, and hearing procedures -- more work for
an always-growing diversocrat cadre. Each newly
recognized problem leads to a call for more programs and staffing."

Campus diversity people have developed their
own professional organization -- the National
Association of Diversity Officers in Higher
Education. They hold annual conferences -- the last
one in Philadelphia. The NADOHE has developed
standards for professional practice and a political agenda, plus a Journal of Diversity in Higher
Education, which is published by the American
Psychological Association.

One wonders just how far spineless college administrators will go when it comes to caving in to the
demands of campus snowflakes who have been
taught that they must be protected against words,
events and deeds that do not fully conform to
their extremely limited, narrow-minded beliefs

built on sheer delusion. Generosity demands that we forgive these precious snowflakes and hope that they eventually grow up. The real problem is with people assumed to be grown-ups — college professors and administrators — who serve their self-interest by tolerating and giving aid and comfort to our aberrant youth. Unless the cycle of promoting and nursing imaginary grievances is ended, diversity bureaucracies will take over our colleges and universities, supplanting altogether the goal of higher education.

"Diversity" is the highest goal of students and professors who openly detest those with whom they disagree. These people support the very antithesis of higher education with their withering attacks on free speech. Both in and out of academia, the content of a man's character is no longer as important as the color of his skin, his sex, his sexual preferences or his political loyalties. That's a vision that spells tragedy for our nation.

-From an article in TownHall magazine by Walter Williams, 1/1/2020.

Those pushing the "tolerable" agenda seldom recognize when they have pushed too far—as in the attitude of the English in the lead-up to the American Revolutionary War. The British hit the colonies with one tax after another; on tea, on sugar, even on an excise tax stamp—refusing to listen to complaints from the colonists. When those cumulative acts became more than the colonists felt obliged to endure, they revolted.

There is a phrase in the Declaration of Independence that should command our attention:

> Prudence, indeed, will dictate that governments long established should not be changed for light and transient causes; and accordingly all experience hath shown that mankind are more disposed to suffer, while evils are sufferable, than to right themselves by abolishing the forms to which they are accustomed. But when a long train of abuses have occurred with disregard for the desires of a sizable group (maybe a majority) deem proper it is their right, it is their duty, to throw off such government, and to provide new guards for their future security.

Tell me you see no commonality between those words and the actions of progressives against those opposed to socialism?

Is separation from one another the only solution available to the two political parties who seem entirely and unalterably opposed to any sort of compromise acceptable to the other side? Indeed, are there several differences wherein one side feels it impossible to compromise?

For instance, if you hold firmly to the belief that it is murder to abort a child moments before that baby could have been delivered in perfect health, how can you reach an agreement? Would the secularists propose to the pro-life group that they accept only, say, 2,000 or 10,000 of those late-term abortions be permitted, but no more? Of course not. All of us must understand that one cannot compromise his or her principles. Even one such death would be too many to tolerate.

To repeat something I've said before, our great-grandchildren might be asking us one day, "Grandfather, how could you have been so callous as to accept the killing of so many millions of unborn children?"

Do we have a ready answer for that question?

> *Today, it is the unborn child; tomorrow, it is likely to be the elderly or those who are incurably ill. Who knows but that a little later it may be anyone who has political or moral views that do not fit into the distorted new order?*
> Dr. Mildred Jefferson, a prominent, outspoken opponent of abortion and the first black woman to graduate from Harvard Medical School.

How about homosexuality and all those other letters of the alphabet that we use to describe sexual deviancy—LBGQT, I believe are the appropriate letters.

Were you aware that for all of recorded history until 1973, homosexuality was considered a psychiatric disorder and an aberrant behavior, even abhorrent? It was listed as a disorder in the American Association of Psychiatrists Diagnostic and Statistical Manual—the *bible* for psychiatrists.

Wikipedia provides a synopsis of sodomy laws in the United States:

> Sodomy laws in the United States, which outlawed a variety of sexual acts, were inherited from colonial laws in the 1600s. While they more often targeted sexual acts between persons of the same sex, there were statutes employed with definitions broad enough to outlaw certain sexual acts between persons of different sexes as well.

All through the 20th century, the gradual liberalization of American sexuality led to the elimination of sodomy laws in most states. *During all this time, however, the Supreme Court upheld the constitutionality of sodomy laws in Bowers v. Hardwick in 1986.*

Historically speaking, that was only yesterday. However, in 2003, the Supreme Court reversed the decision with Lawrence v. Texas, invalidating sodomy laws in the remaining 14 states (Alabama, Florida, Idaho, Kansas, Louisiana, Michigan, Mississippi, Missouri [statewide], North Carolina, Oklahoma, South Carolina, Texas, Utah, and Virginia). Michigan? The only northern state in that list!

So, something deemed denigrating, demeaning and indicative of unnatural feelings for thousands of years was suddenly found to be merely an alternative lifestyle.

What changed in 1973? In her historical overview of homosexuality and its status as a mental disorder ("When Gay Was Not Okay with the APA"), Sarah Baughey-Gill says:

> In 1970, gay rights activists took action and disrupted an APA convention in San Francisco, demanding to be allowed to voice their opinions. As the medical director of the APA at the time, Melvin Sabshin, recalls, there were lots of "hard words" exchanged between protestors and APA members, and it was so disruptive that the APA hired security to ensure order at future meetings. These protests were not ignored, and gay rights activists were allowed to have a gay-focused panel at the 1971 convention in Washington DC. This panel asked that homosexuality be removed from the DSM and tried to explain the stigma caused by the DSM diagnosis. However, although their presence caused a lot of controversy and sparked many

debates, the diagnosis remained. Activists were forced to return again the next year to plead their case to the APA once more.

In his article "Out of DSM: Depathologizing Homosexuality," Jack Drecher writes:

> In any event, the events of 1973 did not immediately end psychiatry's pathologizing (sic) of some presentations of homosexuality. For in "homosexuality's" place, the DSM-II contained a new diagnosis: Sexual Orientation Disturbance (SOD). That new diagnosis regarded homosexuality as an illness if an individual with same-sex attractions found them distressing and wanted to change.

After years of badgering, staging protests, demonstrations and sit-ins at APA conventions by influential groups of homosexuals, the American Psychiatric Association was induced to (or coerced into) holding a vote to decide whether to drop homosexuality, *per se,* from their DSM. The measure was approved by the majority of votes cast, but almost half the psychiatrists boycotted the election and did not vote. Not exactly a ringing endorsement, but we are expected to "soldier on" with the new rules, whether we like them or not.

The bottom line is, if you want to pursue the homosexual lifestyle, by all means do so. However, if you expect that when you are in the company of heterosexual males with teenage boys that you will be treated just like every other male, you should not be surprised when those other men look upon you with antipathy, mistrust and deep suspicion. They may well have a deep aversion to seeing their child groomed and recruited by a homosexual to a lifestyle that will in all probability deny that boy the experience of natural, wholesome lovemaking with a woman.

Then there is the use of terribly offensive language in very public places. Fifty or sixty years ago, use of the f-bomb in public was against the law. It might be grounds for arrest of the perpetrator. It was considered rude, disrespectful and unconscionable for someone to use such a word in the presence of women or children. Now, it is very common in almost any setting.

You see, the loudest, most vociferous among us seem to accomplish their goals, while the average citizen says, "Well, it doesn't really affect me, so I'm not going to stick my neck out to oppose it."

I'd ask you to look at this like the Electoral College, if you will. Without the Electoral College, the voting citizens of California, New York and Texas could dictate to the other forty-seven states the kind of government we would have, and the citizens of those other states would have to "like it or lump it." If you attended high school when history truly was taught, you will have learned that a huge sticking point in forming a United States out of the original 13 colonies was that the other 12 colonies did not want Virginia, far and away the most populous colony at that time, to dictate all terms of union to the rest of the nation. That is why the founders came up with the plan for each state to have representatives apportioned based upon population, but each state would have only 2 senators, selected by their respective state legislatures.

Applying the wisdom of the founders to behaviors, why should the majority of American people who do not use vulgar language in public settings be forced to accept such rude and inconsiderate acts on the part of a minority?

Chapter 16

IS GOOGLE AN ENEMY OF FREE EXPRESSION?

Shelly Sim

Hi, I'm too looking for a balance search engine because yahoo is way off balanced and Google is not balanced and Bing is somewhat off balanced. I can't seem to set my settings for Google or yahoo to send fair and balanced news on the candidates because I get a little tired of seeing news about Trump which half of its false since I was witness to the real story but I'm looking for more info on Hillary scandals from Wikileaks but search engines seem to leave all that out. So if there is a better search engine...please share. Thanks

11/10/2016
Morganisms
Yeah looks like Google is bought and paid for by the current power structure. They skew search results to favor Hilary, just as bad as these horrible news outlets. Pretty shameless what Google is doing in this election.

13/10/2016
StevieD_Web

And yet others are whining about the inclusion of Breitbart and other radical conservative propaganda machines being allowed pixels in the news.

Hmmmm, when both extremes are unhappy, Google must be doing something correct.

All the above are from Google News Help.

ON THE SUBJECT of "tolerance," we are reminded of the complete lack of tolerance for conservatism on the part of those in charge of Facebook, You Tube, Google and all the other means of social network communications.

In an article written on September 7, 2019, Ned Ryan of the Center for American Greatness wrote that Google had just that week announced that they had removed 500,000,000 comments (500 million!), more than 100,000 videos and over 17,000 channels from You Tube. You see, in the absence of any coherent guidance from our elected officials, Google, a private corporation, has decided *it* will be the arbiter of free speech.

Ryan offers the idea that perhaps our elected officials are fools, or alternatively have been "bought off" by Google and others. The only thing certain is that allowing Google to implement this policy is pure idiocy.

In July of this year, Dr. Robert Epstein testified before the U.S. Senate that Google's search-engine manipulation likely swung between 2.6 million and 10.4 million votes to Hillary Clinton in 2016. There is no way to ascertain whether it was done, but *if* Zuckerberg had chosen to send out a simple message like, "Get out the vote!" to Democrats only (Does Google know what party you belong to? Of course, they do!), that alone would have increased Democrat votes by about 450,000, according to Epstein. Also according to Epstein, if Zuckerberg did not send out that 'Get out the vote' email to Democrats only, it was only because he thought Trump had no chance of winning the Presidency; he (Zuckerberg) was over-confident of that 'fact.'

It is Epstein's estimation that if nothing is done to curb Google and other companies in the Silicon Valley, the vote in 2020 might well see a *15 to 20 million vote swing* in favor of the Democratic candidate! Bernie Sanders might well ask, "Well, what's wrong with that?"

Go on Google right now and try to search for a positive opinion about Jesus Christ or Christianity. You will find nothing without some artfully worded questions and determination to find that positive item. You see, the search engine will likely switch you to a site extolling the virtues of agnosticism or atheism, perhaps a homily about the beauty of secularism. Christianity? There is a great deal of negative information but very little good about Christianity on the internet unless you know exactly where to look for it. You will get no help in this regard from the search engine because it is designed to frustrate that effort.

Our country has been all in a-tither about a so-called Russian "information troll farm", the Internet Research Agency (IRA) spending just 0.05 percent as much on Facebook ads as Hillary Clinton and Donald Trump's campaigns combined in the run-up to the 2016 U.S. presidential election. Yes, they did reach a good-sized audience. While there might have been other Russian disinformation groups, the IRA spent $46,000 on pre-election day Facebook ads compared to $81 million spent by Clinton and Trump together, not including political action committees who could have spent even more than that on either campaigns' behalf.

Russia spent all that money allegedly attempting to dissuade voters from voting for Ms. Clinton. Where did the Russians spend this money? On Facebook/Google. I will offer you an iron-clad guarantee that Google did not cooperate with the Russians in this endeavor. In comparison with the shenanigans of Google on Hillary's behalf, the Russian efforts seem like child's play.

The efforts to wreck our election process are serious, but that's not all Google is doing surreptitiously. There are reports coming out of Silicon Valley that "social credit score" systems are being developed for the United States, much as has already been done in China.

What is so bad about that, you ask? What is a "social credit" score?

Think of a "social credit system" in terms of tech companies and corporations creating their own system of right and wrong, their very own moral code they will implement to force citizens into the sort of behavior they feel is "tolerable," based on their worldview and faith system, or absence thereof. It may not be illegal, but it most certainly is extralegal. For the crime of holding views that are contrary to those held by that corporation, you may be charged a higher price for a product you purchase from that company. You may be required to pay a higher interest rate, or—you might not be able to buy their product at all. You will have no right to a jury or judge to adjudicate any appeal you might lodge, if there was even anyone before with whom you might lodge a disagreement. Many things may change if this is allowed to stand.

George Will writes in a syndicated column that China is adopting a "social credit system" in which each person's cumulative commercial and social-media activities give them a score that will determine their access to education, travel, housing, health clinics— just about everything in their lives. China has spent more on this "social credit system," referring to it as "stability maintenance," than on their vaunted military. Oh, guess who helped China develop this system? You got it—Google!

Ma Jian wrote a novel called *China Dream*, in which the main character, Ma Daode, Director of the (so far) fictional China Dream Bureau, is trying to develop an injection of a neural implant into the brain so that all recipients will have the same repetitive dream of the wonders of China. Citizens of Hong Kong have read this book—that's why they are fighting so hard against China's proposal to remove individuals charged with a crime in Hong Kong to China for trial; the so-called "extradition" bill.

Ayn Rand's novel, *Atlas Shrugged,* has her protagonist, John Galt, retiring with other captains of industry to an undisclosed secret canyon somewhere in the western United States. These individuals intend to remain in seclusion, producing no goods and services, until the government accedes to their demand that they be given the right to determine how their goods and services are to be used. What could be wrong in that? After all, they are the producers—shouldn't they have a say as to how their goods are utilized? By the way, Ayn Rand was a secular humanist.

In today's America, if you are from the opposing (conservative) worldview, you might be restricted by the corporations in Silicon Valley and elsewhere, owning such facilities, as to if, when and where you might travel. You might well be refused service at certain restaurants where you might choose to eat. You could be stigmatized, ostracized. Think not? It is happening even as I write this in China.

It gets much worse. Google has also established a company called AI Lab (referring to Artificial Intelligence) in Beijing. Wait until you learn what service this AI lab performs for China, and the fact that Google decided to end its Maven contract with the USA in 2018. What is the Maven contract, you ask?

The *New York Times* reports, "Google, hoping to head off a rebellion by employees upset that the technology (AI) they were working on could be used for lethal purposes (to make drones more effective), will not renew a contract with the Pentagon for artificial intelligence work when a current deal expires next year."

That is the exact same program they are developing for China! So, they will assist China with the development of a lethal system but refuse to offer the same service to their own country. It could be that Beijing is offering more money for that service than the United States is willing to pay. (See the next section—"Unfettered Capitalism.")

There is more to it than that. Xi Jinping in 2017 had added to the Communist Party Constitution the principle of "civil-military fusion," which in essence dictates that *all research done in China must be shared with the People's Liberation Army.* Let's see—would that include the Google research, being done in Beijing? What do you think?

It seems that the leaders of Google have decided that it is "evil" to work with the United States military, but perfectly alright to do business with the Chinese Communists and their military.

Google wants to be the power broker in this country; they want to decide what is and is not accepted speech while freely working with the Chinese Communists who allow almost none of the freedoms America provides its citizens. Perhaps Mark Zuckerberg should ask himself an extremely pertinent question: what will happen to him and his company should America become just like China?

What motivates Zuckerberg and others in positions of ownership and power in the social media sphere? Is it money? Is it power? Is it politics?

We may never find out.

Chapter 17

UNFETTERED CAPITALISM

When most people think of "democracy" they usually mean a constitutionally limited democracy. The function of a limited democracy is to decide who held political power and how that power is specifically exercised (such as how many policemen or judges are needed), but what that power is should be strictly defined and limited in the constitution. (This is basically the original American system.) In a proper capitalist nation, a constitution based upon individual rights would be necessary to limit the actions of its citizens and the government. Under capitalism, the majority would never be able to vote to violate the rights of the minority, no matter how large the majority or how small the minority. Individual rights would not be subject to vote.—
Harper College – Capitalism; FAQ

UNFETTERED CAPITALISM IS little better than socialism. By that I mean that capitalism must have guidelines, parameters within which it may operate. The worst thing in the world, to the socialist, is capitalism. In their eyes, it is an evil, blood-sucking monster that steals from the poor to line the pockets of the rich. If you are not born rich, you are at an irretrievable disadvantage and will forever be in service to the military-industrial complex that controls the country.

While capitalism isn't actually any of those things, I do have some concerns about capitalism as pursued in today's America.

A few years ago, I bought a book by Irving Kristol, the father of William Kristol of *The New Republic* magazine. The title of the book, written by the elder Kristol, intrigued me. It was *Two Cheers for Capitalism.* I purchased it with the expectation that, like me, Mr. Kristol saw the primary flaw in capitalism as practiced in the United States—that it was totally unencumbered by a conscience.

By that I mean that capitalism must have guidelines, parameters within which it must operate. Some of the Founders—specifically, Alexander Hamilton—predicted that all the liberties guaranteed in our American Constitution would provide a temptation, too strong to be controlled for certain individuals, to exercise their freedoms at the expense of others. Freedoms of the sort guaranteed in our constitution have been exploited to enable our courts to call the publication of very explicit pornography, like Larry Flynt's *Hustler* magazine, a legitimate practice of Flynt's freedom of speech.

Huh?

Can the poisoning of the minds of our children be so unimportant to us that we will defend a man's right to publish smut and sell it on newsstands across America so that even pre-teen boys can obtain a copy?

Hustler magazine has to be considered tame now when compared to the sex and violence portrayed on prime-time evening television programming. "Sex sells," say the Hollywood elites. Violence, too, apparently, because that is perhaps 80–90 percent of what passes for entertainment now, in both television and movies. Books, too, unfortunately.

We do have a law in this country making it illegal to shout, "Fire!" in a crowded theater. I fully support that law; people could be trampled to death in a stampede caused by such an irresponsible act.

I also believe that pornography is the bane of our nation. Admittedly, I have seen much more of the ugly underbelly of pornography than most ever see. From my perspective, if we had it in us to be so, we ought to be ashamed. Not to worry—it apparently takes much more than that to provoke shame in us.

As a polygraph examiner, I have had a front row seat from which to observe the degradation in men and families caused by pornography.

You might say, "But Bill, tragedy doesn't follow everybody who views pornography."

That is true. And not every child who plays in a Los Angeles freeway gets run over. However, the odds of such an event happening are far too great for me to willingly take a chance with my child. You may be able to view pornography occasionally and not be adversely affected by it. However, I have spoken with more than 100 men who have struggled with pornography's influence upon them and the destruction it has caused in their lives and families. Enough for me to recommend strongly that you not expose yourself to it at all.

I have seen the lives of small children ruined completely. Most children never recover from being molested before they even know what sex is. They will be emotionally crippled for the rest of their lives, and more than a few of them will choose suicide rather than live with the shame.

Again, I have administered polygraph examinations to men who have told me they spend as much as 8-10 hours a night in their "home office" watching pornography on their computer. They assure me that it's not harmful to anyone but themselves—and they see no real hurt for themselves. I believe that addiction to pornography crowds out almost everything else in a person's life so that it becomes all he thinks about from the time he gets up until he goes to bed. All available money he spends on items to feed his sexual addiction, neglecting his wife and family and often losing his employment because of his preoccupation with smut.

A few of you might remember that in 1970, when the Supreme Court was struggling with a definition for pornography, the temporary decision was to leave it up to "the community" to decide for its own citizens what constituted smut; what is not fit to see or publish. President Richard Nixon appointed a blue-ribbon committee to define pornography and estimate its effect on society. The committee report pooh-poohed the idea that pornography was harmful and suggested in essence that every adult should be free to watch any kind of pornography he wanted.

It was widely reported sometime after the committee was disbanded that a few of the committee members became addicted to pornography; some to the point of having to seek psychiatric help in dealing with the problem.

Do we as a nation have to endure the crassness of smut-peddlers like Larry Flynt and the hundreds more of a similar bent in Hollywood who are the purveyors of films and television programming that appeal to the lowest common denominator of depravity? Do we have to accept this degradation in order to prove that we are "cosmopolitan," and not Puritans or Neanderthals? (Don't you sometimes want to ask, "What's wrong with being a Puritan or Neanderthal man"?)

Oh, but we must have the freedom to voice our opinions—and that right is guaranteed in the First Amendment to the Constitution.

Does the Constitution really say we must tolerate the printing and distribution of pornography or we will be violating someone's rights?

I don't see that in my copy of the Constitution.

You cannot make illegal every act that man could commit against another person. Even if that were possible, you should know that making something illegal does not mean that nobody will ever violate that newly-minted law. For a while, Congress pursued the policy of making every crime with which the nation appeared to find difficulty enforcing a violation of federal law, to be investigated and prosecuted by the FBI. As a result, the FBI caseload doubled, but the rate of crime remained largely undiminished.

As Publius Tacitus opined almost 2,000 years ago, "The more voluminous the laws, the more corrupt the nation."

Laws do not change peoples' hearts. So, what is needed is something that will alter the way citizens view acts that are not in the best interests of all the people. That is where Christianity comes in. Remember what Thomas Jefferson said about Christianity—that it "changes hearts"?

Doing the right thing becomes much more palatable when it is the choice that most people make and is rewarded by wide approval, rather than when refraining from an action is forced upon them by the law. Sometimes we labor under the illusion that *all* people must heartily embrace the idea of better behavior from purer motives in order for it to be effective. That is not true—and it never has been true. The approbation of respected people has a tremendous influence even when their numbers are not large.

It has not always been easy to find ways around the wording of the Constitution. Members of the U.S. Congress, while James Madison was still a member, proposed that the Congress should contribute money to alleviate the suffering of Haitian refugees from the recent French war; undoubtedly a worthy cause. However, Mr. Madison—widely accepted as the primary author of the United States Constitution—demurred.

Of course, that was certainly not the last time Congress was petitioned to contribute the people's money to some worthy cause or another. A problem we have now is in finding a request *against* which Congress can be persuaded to vote. The request is usually couched in language that includes the phrase, "It's for the children."

Somewhere in that Constitution Congress "found" the authority to appropriate these funds—just like the place in the Constitution that they located the right for a woman to abort a viable child. Have you examined the convoluted thinking necessary to justify that "right"?

If you can make sense of the convoluted thinking required to find in that Constitution the right of a woman to abort her baby, the rest of us would appreciate it if you could enlighten us.

It is believed that Vladimir Lenin, one of the principal leaders of the Bolshevik Revolution that overthrew Czarist Russian rule and established a communist government said, "We will hang the capitalists, and they will bid against each other for the privilege of selling us the rope."

Now, *that* would be "rogue capitalism!"

Was Lenin an accurate forecaster? Could he look into the future of the United States and see what would become a very serious problem for us?

Chapter 18

IN FAVOR OF THE CONSTITUTION AND GOOD

*The Constitution is not an instrument for the gov-
ernment to restrain the people, it is an instrument for
the people to restrain the government–lest it come to
dominate our lives and interests.*

– Patrick Henry (disputed)

IF—AND THAT IS a *big* if—Americans do wish to continue
with a democratic republican form of government, how can the
slide to socialism be halted and our people helped to see the value
of freedom and liberty?

Benjamin Franklin once said, "Those who would sacrifice liberty for security will end up having neither."

To some, the prospect of having food, housing, transportation, healthcare and public school education without paying for
any of those things sounds fantastic. And it is; as in "unbelievable."
Again, to some the *quality* of that education, healthcare, etc. is not
as important as that it is *free*. We'll settle for a mediocre education,
a mediocre house and car, and subpar healthcare so long as we don't
have to pay anything at all for those services.

Oh, I don't mean that we will settle for those inferior services
without complaining. If you think all recipients of welfare, food

stamps and other benefits are perfectly satisfied with the services provided them *gratis*, you have not spent much time in an office where welfare recipients meet with their caseworkers and quarrel with them about increasing their allotment. The arguments get heated, if a little unintelligible.

Something we know intellectually but have never bought into as a people and as a nation is that you cannot buy friends. Yes, I am quite aware that the progressives have "owned" the poor and the minorities of our country in a political sense for many years. Do not mistake the fact that they vote Democrat as an indication of infallible love for that party. Perhaps I am entirely wrong, but I believe that in the minds of many of those whose lack of education and absence of a work ethic harbor in their heart of hearts resentment that they have not been treated as adults; have not been afforded an opportunity to fend for themselves, to provide a living for their families by working for a living wage. Certainly, there are quite a number of these that are not satisfied with their situation but afraid to rock the boat for fear it might result in a worsened condition. This is what the progressives have purchased with their "free stuff"— an acquiescence, fragile and grudging. That is why the progressives are leaning more and more toward socialism, so that they can rule without the hassle of having to run for re-election every two, four or six years. Oh, they'll continue to have elections, but they will be like all those elections Venezuela has held in the 20+ years since the election of Hugo Chavez—the result is a foregone conclusion.

What are we creating thereby?

A nation which, more and more, is becoming top-heavy with those who will not or cannot work and who have become entirely dependent upon a reduced number of Americans who can and do work—at least for the time being.

You might have seen this point illustrated with a depiction of a wagon, first with only one or two people on board and a great number pulling the wagon along. Everybody seems happy. The next frame shows that same wagon over-filled with people, and a very few straining very hard to keep forward motion going. The message is clear.

We have become complacent over the years. No, not just complacent. We have been as a flock of sheep, allowing the secular humanists to lead us wherever they want us to go. Urged by the progressives to be "more tolerant" of the views and indeed the actions of others with whom we differ, we have become so tolerant, so malleable to the soft persuasion and reassurances of the humanists that the program(s) they are pushing is/are "for the good of the country" (or for "society", or for the "children") that we have actually lost the ability to be embarrassed or ashamed. If we are ashamed, we keep that to ourselves lest we be ridiculed as right-wing religious zealots for our inability to wink at egregious wrongs.

A recent example of an egregious misdeed was perfectly illustrated by the Speaker of the House of Representatives, Nancy Pelosi, when she accused Republicans of lying to the American public and the press, told a friendly audience that *she had seen Republican candidates for office spread lies about Democrat opponents she was supporting.*

She said, "They tell them a lie about the candidate, the press prints that lie as the truth, then they refer to the articles which were based upon their press release and cite that as proof of the allegations they had made."

Those are supposedly Nancy Pelosi's own words! Have you seen any examples of Republicans using that tactic?

You see, to persuade the media to print a defamatory article about a progressive candidate would seem to require their (the media's) total agreement and full cooperation with the scheme, would it not? When is the last time a mainstream media outlet printed an article favorable to *any* Republican candidate, let alone President Trump?

The exact same method about which Ms. Pelosi spoke **was** used by Christopher Steele to introduce his memo, the so-called 'Steele Dossier,' accusing Donald Trump of colluding with Russian agents to get their help in winning the American presidency. Steele gave a copy of it to Senator John McCain of Arizona, not known to be a confederate of Donald Trump. McCain wrote that it all seemed "too strange a scenario to believe" at first, but eventually decided that "even a remote risk that the President of the United States might be vulnerable to Russian extortion had to be investigated."

The late Sen. John McCain provided intimate details of how he obtained the infamous so-called Steele Dossier in his 2018 book, *The Restless Wave*. He said he met with FBI Director James Comey to give him a copy of all the written material that he had received. I am sure it would be difficult to assemble enough evidence to call it a "hate crime," but Senator McCain's trusted aide, David Kramer, testified that he had given a copy of the Steele Dossier to the *Wall Street Journal*, to Fred Hiatt of the *Washington Post*, to CNN's Carl Bernstein, to National Public Radio, to McClatchy's News Service *and others*.

Steele alleged to the media that there was information floating around that contained certain revelations about Donald Trump supposedly colluding with the Russians to help him win the presidential election of 2016. In January of 2017, Steele gave a copy of the dossier to *Buzz Feed*, who printed information from it. Steele then cited the *Buzz Feed* article as proof of the allegations he had made earlier. Guess what? It worked! Just as Nancy Pelosi had described it! Not as well as progressives would have liked, but it did accomplish a two-year search for mythical collusion between Donald Trump and unnamed Russians.

Similarly, Harry Reid came up with a totally unsubstantiated allegation prior to the 2016 presidential election to the effect that he had come across some information that showed Mitt Romney, the Republican opponent of President Barack Obama, had paid no federal income taxes for the past ten years. The only way for Romney to prove him wrong was to allow the progressives access to those tax returns, and he was not about to do that—as Reid certainly was aware.

When the election was concluded and Barack Obama had won, a reporter asked Harry Reid whether or not he felt bad about making such an outlandish charge against the Republican candidate.

Reid's reply? "Well, he (Romney) isn't president today, is he?" Perfect reasoning in support of his blatantly untruthful charge—the end justifies the means.

But, does it?

Before you burst with admiration for Reid's courage in speaking up about Romney's tax problem, you should be advised that when Reid *directly* accused Romney of being a tax dodger, he did so from the safety of the Senate floor—where he could say almost anything without fear of legal repercussions. Outside the protection of legislative immunity, Reid stated Romney was only *possibly* a tax dodger.

Not only does Reid not think he did anything wrong by that— let's be charitable and call it 'misinformation'—he is actually proud that his lies might have helped cost Romney the election.

By the way, Ashe Schow of the *Washington Examiner* (not the *Washington Post*) first reported Reid's post-election comments. Only after Fox News had run with Schow's story of Reid's callous attitude did other media sources report those misdeeds quoted above. Apparently, it was not deemed 'newsworthy' until the "right-wing" media announced on their networks what Reid's response had been. Not surprisingly, the left-leaning press then agreed that maybe Reid was out of bounds in saying those things.

That use and misuse of the media by the Democrats/progressives, among many other questions, is still up to the American people to decide; at least for one more election. If the extreme progressive wing of the Democratic party wins the coming 2020 elections—and by that I mean the presidency and control of at least one house of Congress—may I make the bold prediction that there will be no more free and democratic elections? We may continue to have "elections"—like Venezuela continues to have "elections"—but they will not express the free will of the people of America.

Does America esteem honesty anymore? That is not a vacuous question. Do you remember how enamored the media became with Bill Clinton when that President's lies confounded his questioners? They even wrote fawningly about how well he lied, or "dissembled," as Clinton called it. So again, do we still have any regard for honesty? You will have seen many instances on television and in print in which you must undoubtedly be convinced that honesty is not one of the attributes our media holds sacrosanct.

Without a high degree of honesty on the part of people involved in the election process, how can American voters have confidence in the announced results? Perhaps if your party is winning, it doesn't matter to you. However, you must keep in mind that whatever you can do to cheat and defraud your enemies, they can do the same or worse to you.

Without the certainty that our stock market is conducted with integrity, how can the average investor be persuaded to risk what little capital he has? If he believes the market is rigged in favor of the billionaire participant and that one can use vast sums of money in the hands of an individual or a hedge fund to drive the market in a direction that will ruin the small investor but will enrich the Warren Buffets, is he going to take part in his own demise? Wouldn't that be a terrible circumstance should these billionaires have to steal from each other rather than from the masses? If those with money to risk have no confidence that they will get a fair shake from the market and not have to take the leavings of insider traders, that money will eventually dry up. We all lose.

How about banking? Would you deposit your money with a bank whose president was a convicted thief?

How about insurance?

Will these businesses thrive if people are fearful that they are being lied to and fleeced for unconscionable profits by dishonest bankers and the purveyors of insurance policies?

How about our public education system? Would you be willing to continue sending your children to a school where they were having their heads filled with erroneous and deliberately false information? Our education system is in plenty of disarray as it is. If you were to discover that teachers and school administrators were lying to you to justify their presence, would you keep your children in that kind of school?

I know you will have heard of a time, and perhaps some of our older readers were fortunate enough to live in such an era, when a handshake was all that was necessary to seal a deal. No lengthy contract. Men did not have to bring their lawyers to a meeting where a deal was expected to be consummated. They simply did not trade with those they could not trust.

How can our justice system continue to survive when there is so little confidence in those attorneys and judges whose job it is to mete out justice? Many honest attorneys know that the integrity of the court is and has been compromised, yet the measures to rectify the worst violations are timid, at best. Some attorneys will openly tell you, "When I know my client is guilty, I'll fight even harder to get an acquittal."

So, has this become just a contest to see who can win in court? When did it cease to be a procedure to sort out the facts and allow justice to prevail? A long time ago, it seems.

If the people have little to no confidence that they are going to be treated fairly by our courts, does that not encourage lying—dissembling—on their part? If you know justice is going to prevail and you are going to be treated fairly you will tend to place your confidence in the outcome and be honest in your testimony. Otherwise, whatever outcome the court has is not going to resemble justice at all.

There are four groups that participate in the system of justice: law enforcement officers, district attorneys or U.S. attorneys and their assistants, defense counsel, and judges. It is incumbent upon all four of these groups to demonstrate a level of honesty and concern for a just outcome that is unassailable. When that becomes the norm, our justice system will run as smooth as clockwork.

Do you think that confidence is there today? No? Why not? Is it because too many people in positions of authority do not hold themselves up to the standards necessary to ensure a just judicial system?

I wish to make a point here, a point that hopefully will become clear later in this narration, that society, whether operating in large groups or small, will produce thoughts and actions which have a strong tendency to emanate from the lowest common denominator.

What do I mean by that?

If you have within almost any group individuals representing both ends of the spectrum, from high intelligence to intellectually challenged, from gentle as a lamb to those whose behavior resembles that of the Marquise de Sade, that group will in most instances emulate the thoughts and actions of the latter in each of the above couplings. They will not follow the wisdom of the more enlightened of their number, nor will they adopt the meekness of the lambs among them. Rather, they will give themselves over to their baser selves and blindly follow those whose instincts lead them to foolish, vile and destructive actions.

Why is that so? *Is* it so?

Should you have the opportunity, you should observe the men and women who serve as police officers for your community. Each Department selects from a roster of applicants the cream of the crop to be inducted and trained to become officers in that Department. Bright men and women all, with a great deal of promise of becoming servants of the people; capable, motivated and dedicated.

Once on the police force, they cannot but be influenced by the more experienced officers, and that for the rookie takes in the entire force. Most of these veterans are excellent officers, good investigators, and fine representatives of the city they serve, excellent in public relations, report writing, and effecting arrests. Their uniforms are clean and pressed, their cars clean and shiny, their attitudes positive and cheery.

Are these the officers the new rookies wish to emulate?

Not often, but *too* frequently, there is another, smaller group of men, usually, who spend a great deal of time in the weight room and who have their shirts tailored to show off to maximum effect their bulging biceps and pectoralis majors. They scoff at the rule book by which their actions are supposed to be directed and brag of having a way that for them is more effective than those rules in the book. Some of these men use such filthy language that it would embarrass a sailor. Their infidelities often lead to divorce and the loss of their families—you get the picture. Yet to too many of the rookies, these men are the epitome of law enforcement; exactly what every officer ought to look like.

Almost all of the rookies will eventually see through the bravado and blustering of these would-be Arnold Schwarzeneggers, and go on to become good, contributing officers, excellent representatives of their city and its citizens. Others lose their dream and lose their jobs before it dawns on them that world they found to be so attractive is not the real one. Their heroes just get a lion's share of the attention; not all of it good.

I'm not picking on police officers. Look at any law enforcement agency, and you will see the same thing: FBI, ATF, State Bureaus of Investigation. The U. S. Army suffers from the inordinate influence of the hell-raisers on the rest of the ordinary soldiers. Football teams are subject to the same problems. The fact is, those we should emulate and follow after, we reject in favor of the more flamboyant problem children. If there are enough of these grown-up children in your department or organization—or in your nation—the problems could be severe.

Why do we not correct that problem?

There's the real rub.

Each generation tries to outdo its predecessors in gentility, tolerance and fairness. Stay with me on this—I promise we will get around to the reason our so-called 'Alpha' males (I actually despise that term) get away with their act. Some of you may remember the times when a young fellow disrupted his class at school, he would be ushered outside the classroom where the 'board of education' would be firmly applied to his posterior. It was actually excellent 'applied psychology.' Often, upon re-entering the classroom, there was ample evidence for the teacher that the lesson had not been lost on the other students. If this tactic was utilized early in the school year, classroom problems were reduced by more than eighty percent. And one or two such punishments were all that needed to be administered—all year.

We can't administer that sort of punishment in today's America. Apparently, corporal punishment, as it was once called, now amounts to a violation of that part of the Constitution which proscribes cruel and unusual punishment. We are no longer that crude or backward. It is always wrong to strike a child, we are informed by those who are supposedly the brightest among us.

If there should be a return to the use of corporal punishment, there must be certain requirements for its application. Number one, it must be administered by a caring teacher. Secondly, both the recipient of the spanking and the class he was interrupting have to know that the reason for the paddling was just and infinitely clear to all—i.e., this activity will not be tolerated in the classroom. As with a lot of things I can think of, the teacher who enjoys paddling students should not be allowed in the classroom. Paddling, as I can personally attest, is a strong deterrent to bad behavior, as long as the child knows it is being handled by a teacher who cares about the child and wants him to benefit from the experience. Never to hurt, always to help that child.

Not all students can profit from a spanking. What then? If we have learned anything from our failures in education, it is that without discipline in the classroom, learning rarely occurs. If someone in that teacher's class is constantly disruptive, belligerent and disrespectful, he must be removed from the class—period. The remainder of the class should not have to pay the price for that single student's disruptive actions.

Teachers among our reading audience will understand this perfectly—the child in your class most in need of love and concern for him or her as a person is almost always the most unlikeable child in class. More often than not, his acting out is a means of getting attention; he just does not know how to get nor how to react to positive attention.

If you cannot punish that child in a physical way, and you cannot remove him permanently from your class, what is left in dealing with a student who just will not cooperate? Sure, he has a right to an education, just like everybody else. But at what price? Truly disruptive students make it impossible for anyone, including himself, to get an education. Going to school should not be like entering a war zone. One should not have to wear an armored vest and a Kevlar helmet to insure his or her personal safety in a public school building. Yet that is exactly how too many students and teachers feel every day. Why do we tolerate that? Because that student has "certain rights".

You see, for the past sixty years in the United States, we have been greatly concerned about "rights"—even manufacturing out of whole cloth rights that had never been conceived before, and finding justification for those rights in the Constitution, of all places. Funny how those who are so concerned about rights care little to be reminded of the responsibilities that must accompany them.

For instance, in 1794, the U. S. House of Representatives appropriated funds to relieve the suffering of French refugees of the revolution on the island of Haiti. (Congress did pass this, over the objections of Madison). In the first time that remarks before the House were quoted verbatim, James Madison made the following remark: "I cannot undertake to lay my finger on that article of the Constitution which granted a right to Congress of expending, on objects of benevolence, the money of their constituents."

Thomas Jefferson had this to say of wealth redistribution:

> To take from one because it is thought that his own industry and that of his father's has acquired too much, in order to spare to others, who, or whose fathers have not exercised equal industry and skill, is to violate arbitrarily the first principle of association—the guarantee to every one of a free exercise of his industry and the fruits acquired by it.

More recently, another brilliant man, George Mason University Professor of Economics Walter Williams said, "If I put my hand in my pocket and draw out money to give to someone else, that's charity. If anyone else puts his hand in my pocket and withdraws money to give to someone else, that's theft—even if it is the government that takes it."

And yet, our nation does tax wage earners above a certain level and uses that money to pay for shelter and sustenance for those who cannot or will not take care of themselves. Somehow, our learned Congressmen found the authority to do that—where? In the Constitution. The author of the Constitution, James Madison, an apparently brilliant attorney and statesman, could not find that authority in his Constitution to tax some citizens for the benefit of other citizens, but Congress did. They are so smart!

Oh, but appropriation of money is not the only jewel "found" in the Constitution.

In Roe vs. Wade, Federal Courts found in the Constitution the right of a woman to abort her child while it is inside her. Under limited circumstances at first, but now a child can apparently be aborted up to a minute before it would have been born a very viable baby. Where did the courts find that authority in the Constitution? Why, under the "substantive" interpretation of the Due Process clause of the 14th Amendment! If the majority of the Supreme Court agrees that not allowing a woman to abort her child is a violation of that "due process" clause, then it is a violation—period.

Where, in the Constitution, is *anything* said about abortion? That's easy. Nowhere.

Should you ever decide that you want to kill someone, you should remember to be laughing heartily when you commit the act, to avoid an additional charge of "hate crime" to the already serious violation of murder. Why? Is the person more dead if you disliked him than if you were good friends at the time you did him in? Congress so believes, and thus it is the law. Some would call that ludicrous.

You see, we have passed innumerable laws and had hundreds of court decisions which ostensibly increase the rights of one group or another of U.S. citizens. What each of these bits of legislation, including that done by the Supreme Court, have in common is that one group of Americans is aided *at the expense of* another or others.

It is believed by some that the poor benefit from welfare. In order for that benefit to be available, the less poor must pay for that increase in the former group's standard of living by having higher taxes levied upon them, thereby lowering their financial viability.

Perhaps a woman benefits from the ability to abort a child, but no one would say the child's rights are equally protected. Oh, I understand that a fetus is not a child in the eyes of the courts now, but the law is fickle; what is legal today by virtue of some hidden right found in the Constitution, may be declared illegal tomorrow by a more conservative court which could miraculously find support for their views in that same document.

The purpose of the law regarding hate crime, I suppose, was to protect minorities, women, homosexuals, and a plethora of others from being injured or killed because someone hates them. So if anyone benefits, it would be this so-called "protected group." The person who might be convicted of a hate crime—Well, his rights are not seen to be equal. Of course, some of you might think that murder is already illegal, and may ask how can you make the crime of taking someone's life *more* illegal? Well, Congress found a way.

We could go on. We had affirmative action to aid more blacks in procuring a college education. More blacks were admitted to college even though their SAT scores were lower that of other applicants. Who got hurt in that one? If you say whites, you are only partially correct. The real losers are the Asian students. If entrance to institutions of higher learning was based entirely on high school grades and SAT scores, there would be many more Asian students in medical school and law school. So their loss is more severe than that of the whites. What is their remedy for this undoubted discrimination? They have none!

Why not?

The answer is simple. Asians are not a large monolithic voting bloc in America. It is as simple as that.

Are you beginning to get the idea that our government, though proscribed from such activity by the Constitution, chooses winners and losers? Who are the only consistent winners in all these laws passed by Congress? Congress, of course. Because you see, they exempt themselves from having to comply with most of the laws that govern the lives of the simple folk. In a manner of speaking, the Congress is a Super class, above the law, and those of us who work for a living are second-class citizens. You forget that salient fact at your own peril. You thought congressmen were 'servants of the people'? How quaint.

So... We have majored in the United States in the extension of—I wanted to write newly-minted rights, but let us refer to them by the more generous term of "recently discovered" rights—to a select group or groups of people. Some might refer to that as "picking winners and losers." Congress and the Supreme Court will tell you that they are not forgetting responsibilities in these new-found laws. No, the 'responsibility' part comes when they tell *you*, the regular citizen, that, like it or not, *you* have the responsibility of obeying the new laws. Do the victims of crimes alleged to be 'hate' crimes have to demonstrate that he is the totally innocent victim, and that he had no hand in agitating his alleged assailant to the point that physical attack was the only reasonable option available to him? That is not clear. Is it possible that the victim makes remarks about the person who eventually becomes the assailant that were designed to be hateful, even dare him to assault him? As far as I can ascertain, there is nothing in the law as written that makes it imperative for prosecutors/investigators to consider that aspect.

Someone astutely observed recently that for the Congressman, job one is re-election to office. Job two—raising money to campaign for office at the end of his term. Job three—refer back to job one.

I wish those environmentalists so anxious about saving the spotted owl or some frog from extinction would show a similar concern for another endangered species—the American Statesman; another category of beings in imminent danger of being completely obliterated.

What is a statesman? Merriam-Webster has this to say:

1: one versed in the principles or art of government especially: one actively engaged in conducting the business of a government or in shaping its policies

2: a wise, skillful, and respected political leader

Ah, there are 535 men and women who fit the first description, in both houses of congress. However, those who today match all three of the descriptors enumerated in part two of the above definitions are as rare as hen's teeth.

Why is there such a paucity of statesmen?

We've asked a similar question a number of times. Let us rephrase it: Why is there such a scarcity of men and women for whom it is a part of their very being to possess the characteristics of honesty, integrity, courage, faith, concern—dare I say love for his fellowman and the will to do that which is right, regardless of personal interests?

Since time immemorial there have been those who would lie, cheat, steal—do anything in the world to satisfy their wants and desires. At times throughout history, these drags upon society have seemed to outnumber the kind people who worked for a living, were generous with what they earned, and taught their children to do the right thing by everyone and not to think higher of themselves than of their neighbors. Good citizens, who set a proper example for others to emulate. There were enough of these kinds of folks and they possessed the requisite amount of influence to sort of add leaven to the bread of society, in a manner of speaking. These individuals exhibited the characteristics that all men, deep in their hearts, know are correct and just. While often the ones who embodied the attributes of kindness, goodness, generosity, courage and love for their fellowman were not wealthy nor did they have vast landholdings or a title, they somehow exerted an inordinate amount of influence over those who did wield power.

Since the beginning of time as measured *Anno Domini,* during those times when man was on his best behavior, crime and poverty were lessened and most people within the land(s) affected lived relatively happy lives. In almost every instance, this type of "good" times can almost inevitably be traced to periods of spiritual revival in their land.

Chapter 19

POLITICAL CORRUPTION

"[Montesquieu wrote in Spirit of the Laws, VIII,c.12:]
'When once a republic is corrupted, there is no possi-
bility of remedying any of the growing evils but by
removing the corruption and restoring its lost prin-
ciples; every other correction is either useless or a
new evil.'"

—*Thomas* Jefferson: copied into his
Commonplace Book.

THERE HAS BEEN a marked failure in American politics. How did we get to this point wherein things we were taught in the 1940s and '50s were right and good and just have now become wrong and bad and indicative of a biased, dogmatic, priggish, bigoted and unjust character?

Corruption in politics did not begin with the Presidential administration of Bill Clinton. However, one would be hard-pressed to find an earlier administration that more openly disregarded the norms of propriety, morality and legality and conducted business exactly as they wanted. It did not take President Clinton long to "learn the ropes," so to speak. His stint as Governor of Arkansas was obviously a valuable tutorial for the way he intended to operate as President.

For one particularly egregious example, let's examine the sale / gift by the Loral Communications and Satellite Company of a super-secret guidance system they had developed for American inter-stellar rockets—to China!

By way of background, after the disastrous National Aeronautics and Space Administration's (NASA) Challenger launch in 1986 in which three astronauts died, the United States Government decided it would no longer provide delivery service for the various companies in this nation who wished to launch communication satellites. Supposedly, they did not want the financial responsibility in the event of another failure. That left these companies scrambling to find another source to carry their satellites into orbit. They contracted with European governments and the Chinese to perform that task for them—at sometimes outrageous prices.

In 1994, the Chinese approached the group called ITAR (The International Telecommunications Satellite Organization or ITSO), an intergovernmental organization charged with seeing to it "All nations should have access to satellite communications." The Chinese proposed to give a communication satellite a ride into outer space for the ridiculously low price of $56 million—about half the cost of the European's Ariane launch.

Perhaps this is one instance in which America should have "looked a gift horse in the mouth."

Disaster at Xichang

An eyewitness speaks publicly for the first time. – Anatoly Zak.

That is the principle reason that on February 15, 1996, the Chinese attempted to launch a Long March 3B rocket bearing an Intelstat 708 telecommunications satellite manufactured by Loral

Space Systems into orbit. Loral is an American company, at that time headed by a man by the name of Bernard Schwartz.

The U S Department of State had the responsibility for approving any sale, transfer or other use of American military material. When Loral and Hughes requested permission to launch their satellite on a Chinese rocket, the State Department refused that permission, citing the fact that guidance systems in the Loral satellite had potential military usage.

No problem. President Clinton transferred responsibility for the use of Chinese rockets for the launch of Loral's satellite to the Department of Commerce—run by Clinton crony Ron Brown. Permission was quickly obtained from this Department, and Loral proceeded with its launch. See how easy it is?

Shortly before the launch, American support personnel noticed several hundred local citizens standing near the launch area. The Americans were removed a safe distance from the area, for good reason, as it turned out. When the Americans left to get a safe distance from the launch site, there were hundreds of Chinese villagers—onlookers—standing much too close, in the minds of the Americans. When the rocket was ignited, it immediately went off-course and crashed. The area around the gate, where the Chinese people had stood, looked like a war zone. Everything was destroyed and/or burned.

The Chinese officially reported only six dead and another 57 wounded. Americans thought that number of dead could have been in the hundreds. It would not have been possible for all those people to have been evacuated in the time between when they were seen by American observers and when the launch was made. Of course, the Chinese kept all foreigners from the site—for "safety reasons".

An American technician employed by Astrotech to help supervise the launch visited the crash site the next morning, even though they had been advised by American authorities not to assist the

Chinese in the clean-up operation. His main goal was to see to it that if there were any working parts of the satellite that had not been destroyed these parts were secured in American hands. Intelstat 708 contained sophisticated communication and encryption technology they did not want to wind up in the hands of the Chinese. Chinese soldiers surrounded the perimeter to keep the locals from stealing any of the debris. Campbell recalls they were going along the site with their Chinese counterparts, saying, "This is ours, and that is yours." Campbell was surprised how much of the satellite had survived the crash. The propellant tanks were okay, solar panels, a liquid apogee motor and much of the structure were salvaged and packed up for shipment back to the U. S.

The U. S. Department of Defense initially reported that their team had succeeded in recovering the Satellite's encryption/decryption equipment. It turned out that, no, the most sensitive FAC-3R circuit boards were *not* recovered. However, DOD reported these " . . . were mounted near the hydrazine propellant tanks and *most likely* were destroyed in the explosion."

The National Security Agency was not worried because the FAC 3R boards on 708 were uniquely keyed, they said, and even if they were recovered intact by someone else, they would pose no threat to future satellite systems.

Did the Chinese get there first and remove those sensitive parts before the Americans arrived on the scene of the crash? We will probably never know.

What we do know is that a Review Committee with scientists and engineers from several nations and which included Chinese representatives held an inquiry as to the cause of the launch failure. It is possible that it is only coincidental that the Long March 3B rocket has experienced only one partial failure since that Review Committee issued its findings, after having several disasters previously. *Chalk up one free (?) gift the Chinese received from the United States, Loral, and President Clinton.*

I believe one could say without fear of serious contradiction that the Chinese, during the administration of Bill Clinton, got much more from the United States than our nation ever got from them. Former President Clinton may have personally received benefits that he did not share with the rest of us.

In the interim between the investigation of the failure at Xichang and the successful next launch of a satellite, Loral, Astrotech, and others assisted the Chinese in making "corrections" to the Long March 3B rocket, which was notoriously unreliable.

The Chinese thought they knew what had caused the disaster at Xichang, and announced plans to correct it. The companies that insured the payloads the Chinese rockets were to carry insisted that an Independent Review Committee study the problem more thoroughly before they would affix their imprimatur to further launches. Participating were American companies Loral, Hughes and others in the aerospace industry. Apparently, nobody from the U. S. Departments of State or Defense spoke to the American participants about the danger of revealing highly classified information while taking part in the investigation of the causes of the Xichang failure. In May of 1996, they issued a report that contradicted the opinion of the Chinese, who then changed their findings to match the report.

In 1997, The U. S. Defense Technology Security Administration issued a report that China had *benefited significantly from that Review Committee Report* and could improve not only their launch vehicle but also ballistic missiles and in particular ***their guidance systems.*** In 1998, in a classic illustration of locking the barn door after the mule has made its escape, the U. S. Congress reclassified satellite technology as a munition, and put it back under the control of the Department of Defense, rather than Clinton's choice of the Department of Commerce.

In 2002, Loral paid $20 million in fines and compliance expenses to settle allegations of violating export control regulations. Cheap at twice the price.

No export licenses to China have been issued since 1996, and an official at the Bureau of Industry and Security emphasized in 2016 that "no U.S.-origin content, regardless of significance, regardless of whether it's incorporated into a foreign-made item, can go to China."

The Loral company provided a great deal of assistance to the Chinese in preparation for their next satellite launch—including all the information that country needed in order to be able to duplicate the guidance system that was the exclusive property of Loral Communications *and against the law for that company to sell or give to a foreign government.* Loral admitted providing the Chinese all this highly classified information, but stated, "It was an accident. A clerical employee accidentally sent that information to the PRC." It would have been more accurate to have described the recipients of that information as the Communist Party of China.

It would be much easier to believe that any assistance given to China was purely coincidental and accidental were it not for the fact that the Loral Communications and Satellite CEO, Bernard Schwartz, had been the single largest contributor to the Clinton presidential campaign. Schwartz was also in the White House a number of times during State visits by foreign dignitaries (though never Chinese) and was invited to sleep in the White House Lincoln Bedroom on two occasions.

Clinton's "impartiality" would also be easier to accept had it not been for the extraordinary efforts he had made on behalf of Loral to get their satellite into orbit. Perhaps he would have done it if Schwartz had not given a dollar to the Clinton campaign; you can be the judge of that. Subsequent actions of Bill Clinton would also allow a reasonable person to believe that he could have been a thoroughly corrupt, amoral individual, obsessed with sex, money and power. He facilitated the transfer of highly secret information of extreme military value to a country that has been at best a "competitor"—some would describe China as an "enemy" of the United States, though not necessarily of the American President. What would compel a President to act in that manner? This might have been the largest single sell-out of America in recorded history. Benedict Arnold was a piker when it comes to traitorous acts.

I refer you to the remark made by Vladimir Lenin regarding American Capitalism: "We will hang the Capitalists, and they will bid against each other for the privilege of selling us the rope." Was Bill Clinton the auctioneer?

Clinton's actions should not have come as a surprise to anyone who follows politics.

Bill Clinton, when he was Governor of Arkansas, joined a group calling themselves the Democrat Leadership Council (DLC), started in the late 1960s as an effort to bring the Democratic Party back from what was considered too far left. They had lost the last two races for the Presidency by landslide margins after having selected Walter Mondale and George McGovern, respectively, as their candidates.

The DLC started as a group of forty-three elected officials and two staffers, Al From and Will Marshall, who shared their predecessor's goal of reclaiming the Democratic Party from the left's influence, prevalent since the late 1960s. Their focus eventually became to secure the 1988 presidential nomination of a southern conservative Democrat such as Senator (Sam) Nunn of Georgia or Senator (Charles) Robb of Virginia.

Bill Clinton was elected president of the DLC as a moderate Democrat in 1991 while he was serving as Governor of Arkansas. The idea was to bring the Democrats back from the fringe of the left so that they could win national—and particularly Presidential—elections. Rather than either Nunn or Robb, however, *Clinton* became the surprise nominee to lead the Democrat slate of candidates. It is believed that he had the fulsome support of the DLC president.

Democrats rallied behind his candidacy, but Clinton's selection almost immediately placed the leadership of the Democrat Party in what could (should) have been an untenable position as stories came out about his having several trysts with many different women. Allegations began to surface almost immediately.

When all the allegations of sexual and fiscal misconduct were first levied at the Clintons, the Democrat Party was faced with a dilemma. They could either pursue the accusations to find out the truth, as they had correctly done in the instance of accusations that Republican President Richard Nixon had been involved in nefarious misdeeds in the early 1970s. Or . . . they could attempt to brazen it out and defend the President from these "spurious allegations."

We do not know how mightily the Democrats struggled with that decision. What we do know now is that *if* the Democrats did not *sell*, at the very least they *pawned* their collective soul to the Devil in order to maintain Clinton in office.

You would probably have to be eligible for Social Security to remember an excellent old movie entitled, *Damn Yankees*. It starred Ray Walton, Gwen Verdon and Tab Hunter. The gist of the story is that an aging Washington Senators baseball fan named Joe Boyd hated the New York Yankees so badly that he agreed to sell his soul to Satan in exchange for allowing his favorite team, the Washington Senators, to defeat the Yankees in a World Series. Joe Boyd was magically transformed by Satan into a fantastic player for the Senators named Joe Hardy (played by Tab Hunter). Weeks later, when Joe Boyd began missing his wife and had second thoughts about the bargain he had struck, Satan (Walton) introduced a temptress (Verdon) named Lola whose job it was to make Hunter live up to his part of the deal. This siren sang a very sexy song to Boyd: "Whatever Lola wants, Lola gets!"

In the movie, this time "Lola" lost out.

In real life, the Democratic Party and the mainstream media—that sounds like an echo; they DO echo each other, don't they? The only question is, who leads? Does the Democratic Party start the day's talking points, or does the MSM do that? You know, Winston Churchill once said, "If we agree on everything, one of us is unnecessary." Now, all the Democrat leadership and the MSM need to decide is, "Which one of us is unnecessary"? Anyway, both those groups have the role of the Joe Boyd facing temptation, and in this real-life version of the story, Lucifer was the victor.

The assignment of the other parts in our little diorama we will leave to your imagination. Suffice to say that the Democrat Party and the Mainstream Media sold their collective soul to the Devil in exchange for protecting President Clinton. They shielded him, lied for him, and irreparably damaged the reputations of hundreds of people *and of the office of the Presidency* for the sole purpose of maintaining Bill Clinton in office; at whatever cost. Of course, an honorable man would have resigned in the face of all those accusations—as Richard Nixon did in 1974. Let us be clear—Nixon's resignation probably had more to do with his certainty that the Senators in *his own party* would vote to convict him of the impeachment charges and remove him from office. This was a predicament Clinton did not have to worry about with a Democrat majority in the U. S. Senate. Nonetheless, Nixon's resignation saved the country an embarrassing spectacle. It demonstrates remarkable *hubris* that the Democrats now are trying to position themselves as the party with the "high moral ground."

They accepted so much wrongdoing and evil from Clinton that they no longer have a guide by which ethical, moral—even legal—conduct can be measured. If what Clinton did was OK, how can their party be critical of any aberrant conduct by a Democrat? The same yardstick, of course, does not apply to conservatives. Saul Alinsky dictated in his book, *Rules for Radicals*, "Hold your enemy to his exacting standards." Well, the Democrats are holding Republicans to the high standards that they claim to live by. Any deviation from those standards on the part of a conservative results in a verbal crucifixion. For a Progressive... If you have no stated, recorded principles, how can you violate them? Admittedly, you seldom hear a Democrat describe himself/herself as a "committed Christian."

Another major failure on the part of President Clinton was the sort of renegade capitalism that permitted the sale of that highly classified Loral guidance system to China. It was a shortcoming born of a lack of character and an absence of patriotism towards his own country. We should definitely add a further cause for this egregious sell-out; that would be greed; avarice.

Clinton surely was not the first to lie about himself to get elected, but he turned out to be a totally different person from the one he portrayed to voters pre-election. Pragmatic? Yes. Politically savvy? For the most part, yes. Moderate? No. Principled? An emphatic, "No." It has been said that Bill Clinton was a highly intelligent man. I offer evidence to the contrary. A truly intelligent man realizes his areas of weakness and tries to fill those gaps by appointing or hiring smart people with expertise in those areas of the leader's weakness. A foolish man surrounds himself with sycophants who never see that the emperor has on no clothing and are thus unable to give him useful advice that might have salvaged his presidency.

One thing the Clinton Presidency did demonstrate is that in future elections, voters would be well advised to concentrate on selecting a candidate of *character* for the role. By that, I mean someone who is honest, trustworthy, and courageous—a man or woman of integrity, who has demonstrated those attributes all of his/her adult life. It would be helpful should the mass media show any interest at all in the character of Democratic candidates. They flush out any wrongdoing a Republican might have engaged in since the age of six but show little interest in digging for any negative information on a member of their own party.

Character, in my opinion, does not dictate so much what an individual might do as make him aware of what his core character will not permit him to do. That is, if you believe in your very center that you are an honest man, that character that you have established within yourself (with the assistance of your parents, other members of your extended family, teachers, coaches, pastors and peers) *dictates* that your behavior *match that character*. Your emotional well-being depends upon your conduct and speech fitting well with what you believe yourself to be.

When those two do not match—your belief about yourself and your speech and actions—there is a part of your mind that is very uncomfortable with this new and disturbing behavior. Metaphorically, it asks, "What's that new guy doing in here? I don't think I like him at all." Your mind has developed an expectation that each time you are faced with a set of circumstances, you will respond in the same, comfortable way. When you do not, the mind asks itself, what is going on? You become anxious and/or depressed because this is not the way you have resolved such problems in the past.

The solution? Well, many psychiatrists and psychologists would prescribe Paxil or Wellbutrin (those are old medications, not prescribed often these days) to help you over the present problem. However, the only cure with that kind of anxiety/depression is... Get back into the behavior that once was automatic for you and make it once again your default response.

So... a person of good character can be depended upon (usually) to behave in a manner commensurate with what he believes himself to be and that his behaviors have demonstrated for most of his life. Certainly, a person with an excellent character, illustrated by a life that has been lived out and demonstrated those attributes of character every day, is a much better bet than one who neither claims nor has demonstrated a good character in any aspect of his life.

Betting on character is a great deal better than voting for an individual because he is charismatic and has a smooth presentation plus good looks.

Ross Perot, a man many Republicans have never forgiven for running against sitting President George H. W. Bush in 1992, was nevertheless a very successful businessman and a man of high principles. Republicans blame Perot for his having taken 18 percent of the Republican vote from Bush, allowing Bill Clinton to win.

In any event, Ross Perot, who ran a multi-million-dollar business, once told his son, Ross Jr., "Son, employ only men and women of character. We can teach them how to perform the job, but if they are not honest by the time they get to us, it is likely too late for us to teach that."

He was right, and we know it.

Meanwhile, in San Francisco, the Democratic National Committee proudly adopted a resolution on August 24, 2019 hailing the "religiously unaffiliated" as the "largest religious group within the Democratic Party, growing from 19 percent in 2007 to one in three today."

That's great news for those Democrats who would love to replace worship of God with worship of the state.

The DNC resolution declares "that morals, values, and patriotism are not unique to any particular religion, and are not necessarily reliant on having a religious worldview at all." That fits in well with the refusal of the 2016 Democrat Convention to reverse a decision made in 2012 to delete a reference to God from the Democrat platform. When called upon to approve the addition of that omitted portion, the members responded with a resounding "No!"—twice! The moderator ruled that the response had been "Aye," but nobody present or listening and watching on television believed that.

Oh. That's right; the secular humanist sees himself as his own god.

If you are not a secular humanist, what are you doing in the Democrat Party?

Sadly, it isn't just the Democrat Party that is a problem. It is the whole of Congress; not simply because they cannot agree on anything. Wait—that is not completely true. One thing upon which all members of both houses of Congress seem to agree completely is that they are the American elite; the only "royalty" we have in this nation.

As a bit of information about the efficacy of the Democrat Party that you might find interesting, here is a list of the 10 most rat-infested cities in America, according to www.orkin.com.

1. Chicago, Illinois.
2. Los Angeles, California.
3. New York City, New York.
4. Washington, District of Colombia.
5. San Francisco/Oakland/San Jose, California.
6. Detroit, Michigan.
7. Cleveland, Ohio.
8. Minneapolis-St. Paul, Minnesota.
9. Philadelphia, Pennsylvania.
10. Atlanta, Georgia.

Then there are the 10 most dangerous cities in the US, according to Forbes Magazine.

1. Detroit, Michigan.
2. St. Louis, Missouri.
3. Oakland, California.

4. Memphis, Tennessee.
5. Birmingham, Alabama.
6. Atlanta, Georgia.
7. Baltimore, Maryland.
8. Stockton, California.
9. Cleveland, Ohio.
10. Buffalo, New York.

How did Chicago not qualify for that list?

What do each of these cities have in common besides the fact that some of them appear on both lists? ALL of them are run by **Democratic** Mayors. Chicago has not had Republican leadership since 1927, Philadelphia since 1952.

While the Progressive leadership of Los Angeles and San Francisco cannot seem to manage the homeless problem and its attendant defecating in the street, the Governor of Texas, after giving a warning to the Democratic Mayor of Austin, Texas, sent the Department of Transportation into the City to clean up the mess and to displace the homeless.

Chapter 20

WITH FRIENDS LIKE CONGRESS WHO NEEDS ENEMIES?

"One useless man is a shame,
Two is a law firm, and
Three is a congress"—
John Adams, 2ⁿᵈ U.S. President

OUR GREAT CONSTITUTION set up a government of three distinct branches: Executive, Judicial and Congressional or Legislative. They should not be held accountable for the fact that a considerable number of participants in each of those branches would be motivated by personal, political or other sympathies inimical to the United States they were elected or, in the case of the Judiciary, appointed to serve and protect. The expectation was that the American people would not support with their votes an individual whose primary goal would be the destruction of the kind of government envisioned by the founders. When an individual enlists in the United States Army, he is obliged to take the following oath:

I, (name), do solemnly swear (or affirm) that I will
support and defend the Constitution of the United
States against all enemies, foreign and domestic;
that I will bear true faith and allegiance to the same;

*and that I will obey the orders of the President of the
United States and the orders of the officers appointed.*

A man or woman who serves as a police officer will take an oath
similar to this:

*I, [name], do solemnly swear (or affirm) that I will
support and defend the Constitution of the United
States against all enemies, foreign and domestic; that
I will bear true faith and allegiance to the same; that
I take this obligation freely, without any mental reservation or purpose of evasion; and that I will well and
faithfully discharge the duties of the office on which I
am about to enter. So help me God.*

Individuals elected to serve in the Congress or the Senate of the
United States are supposed to take the following oath:

*I do solemnly swear (or affirm) that I will support
and defend the Constitution of the United States
against all enemies, foreign and domestic; that I will
bear true faith and allegiance to the same; that I take
this obligation freely, without any mental reservation
or purpose of evasion; and that I will well and faithfully discharge the duties of the office on which I am
about to enter: So help me God.*

Do you find it interesting that the thing to which fealty is
pledged is not the United States, per se, but is to the *Constitution*
of the United States?

Thirty-three amendments to the United States Constitution
have been proposed by the United States Congress and sent to the

states for ratification since the Constitution was put into operation on March 4, 1789. There is a process in place to introduce proposed changes to the Constitution. It is not a simple process, nor should it be. Changes to such a venerable document should certainly not be undertaken on a whim—the proposal should be widely debated and ratified by the requisite number of states. Absent the lawful amendment of that Constitution, it is now the law of the land, and each military member, law enforcement officer, Senator or House Member has taken an oath to "protect and defend" that Constitution. Not the constitution you might wish for; the one currently in place as the law of the land.

In addition to the requirement that the Congressman "protect and defend" the Constitution, he is also expected to serve the people—of the United States, first—and then of the constituents who sent him to Washington.

Are either of those responsibilities being met? That is a rhetorical question. You could not get Congress to agree on anything—not even what would be in the best interests of the greatest number of Americans. It is not out of line to posit the question: How many of our Senators and Representatives actually care what America needs or wants? Even if you have difficulty with addition, it would probably still be unnecessary to take off your shoes to enumerate the members of the Congress who truly care about their constituents.

Many of you can easily recall the train wreck that brought on the second "Great Depression" in 2008-2009. If you do, you will also recall that it was completely avoidable; Congress knew the cause of the coming bust and what was necessary to prevent it, but they did nothing. Indeed, Senator Barney Franks told the Congress that all was well with the two quasi-government-supported lending institutions. Fannie Mae and Freddie Mac were in no financial difficulty and were doing, "just fine." It was Congress who dictated to American banks and lending institutions that those of extremely limited means and zero credit history were to be provided loans way beyond their ability to repay so that they, too, might become "homeowners." Then the banks could hold the mortgages themselves (the better, safer ones) and bundle the others to be sold to Fannie Mae or Freddie Mac. Congress—not greedy banks—was the principal cause of the credit bubble bursting. Then to make up for their complicity, they voted to bail out the lending institutions that lost their shirts as a result of following the explicit directions of Congress into bankruptcy.

I am not suggesting that was a deliberate act for the specific purpose of turning the American voters against the admittedly feckless George W. Bush and the conservatives, but you must admit it did not hurt the chances of Barack Obama to win the Presidency. Of course, there was more to it than what we have stated so simply, but the credit crisis for which Congress must take full ownership certainly aided the Progressives and Obama.

The reason I bring up the bursting of the real estate bubble is to point out the callousness of our Congressmen.

Did you hear any of them assume any of the blame for that disaster? Did a single one of them say anything to the effect that it was a terrible thing to have been visited upon the American citizen?

I'll answer both those questions. Of course, you did not. Another question of a rhetorical nature is, I wonder how many of those congressmen had to pay a price in any way for their complicity in an imminently avoidable crash? You see, almost all the laws that the House of Representatives and the Senate have passed over the past several years have an exclusion clause—*it does not apply to any member of Congress.*

Another factor to be considered: Since Congress and President Obama decided collectively that the big banks and lending institutions, which were, after all, only following the directions that Congress imposed upon them and had no responsibility for the, uh, you might say *planned failure*, those lending institutions would, of course, have to be reimbursed for their losses. So, for the most part, the lenders did not suffer from that crash. Congress didn't suffer. President Obama didn't suffer. The big banks did not suffer. Who did suffer?

The taxpayer, of course. Did you get a thorough explanation as to why the banks should not have to pay for their perfidious lending practices? No? Or why Congress played what was in essence a dirty trick on the American poor by giving them the hope of a home of their own and then yanking it violently out from under them? Shameful!

So, of all the participants in this fiasco—the Congress, the President, the lending institutions and the citizens of this great nation—only one group/individual had no responsibility for the failure. It is only right that *that* group—the American taxpayer—should take it in the shorts, and that the others should escape all assignment of blame. Neat how the politicians accomplish that every time.

Are these the actions of caring public servants? No. What it shows is Congress' complete disdain and contempt for those who send them to Washington to represent their interests.

Why are these "public servants" so dismissive of their responsibilities, and of us the neglected souls who elected them?

They don't care. They. Just. Don't. Care. This has to change—if we are going to retain our democratic republic.

What the Founding Fathers knew—*knew*—was that with the many freedoms provided in our Constitution, a high degree of self-discipline would be required of all Americans, but particularly those whose position makes abuse of the powers they hold in trust not only possible but likely unless they were imbued with a degree of maturity and concern for the rights of the citizens they represented to guide them every moment of every day. Theirs is a tremendous responsibility, but many of our Representatives and Senators seem to grasp only the perquisites that accompany their high office. By the way, more than half the members of Congress, both House and Senate, are millionaires. Don't tell me that surprises you.

If a majority were truly compassionate towards the people they represent, there should have been remorse for the crash of 2008 and 2009, which, as we have pointed out, was entirely preventable. Did you see any sign that our Congressmen understood and regretted their part in the terrible financial carnage caused by irrational loans which they directed be made solely for the purpose of winning the votes of the poor? Had they genuinely cared for the poor they ostensibly love so much, they could not have suggested that they be set up for failure and loss of the houses they were foolishly/cruelly allowed to purchase. It is sort of like giving your child on Christmas the red wagon he had so often prayed and pleaded for, taking him for a magnificent ride in it, and then yanking it away from him. Better that he had never seen the red wagon than have it cruelly taken from him.

The poor person—indeed, all Americans—might be justified in thinking, *"With friends like these Congressmen, who needs enemies?"*

As much damage as they have inflicted upon our democratic republic, they are certainly not the only obstacle we face.

Chapter 21

COMMUNISM/SOCIALISM

Leftists are seemingly more committed to their goals of fundamentally transforming America than conservatives are to preserving it.
— **David Limbaugh,** *Exposing the Fraud of Socialism.*

OPPOSITION TO THE Christian religion is not the exclusive province of the Progressive party and the secular humanist. While those two groups protest that they have no real affinity for communism, they are truly in lockstep with Putin of Russia, Castro of Cuba and other malevolent world leaders when it comes to their rejection of Christianity and Capitalism.

What about Communism, or its little sister, Socialism, as a basis for a just and sustainable society and government?

Referring to socialism as the 'little sister' of communism is only an adaptation of what Vladimir Lenin said in explaining that, "Socialism is only a first step to communism." He should know.

How has communism fared in its many attempts in countries around the world?

When the next-to-largest communist government, the Union of Soviet Socialist Republics (USSR), was competing with the United States to ascertain which country could build the largest stockpile of nuclear devices and other weapons of war, the Soviet Union found that it could not keep up with American production and innovation. You see, when the government controls not only the means of production (factories, farms, etc.) but the number and kinds of products to be manufactured or crops to be grown, you have a big problem. Those decisions are made by committees, most of whose members have no experience in the fields of endeavor in which they are providing guidance.

For instance, the committee in charge of determining what kind of clothing a factory might produce also have the say in what kind of material to be used, colors, sizes—the whole enchilada—with no useful market survey to ascertain whether the people might want to purchase that kind of clothing. As a result, a factory might manufacture 20,000 suits made of a rough serge material in, say, a dull gray color, all in size 40 regular. If you have ever worked with committees, you will be able to understand how this can happen. Remember, committee appointments are based on party loyalty or personal loyalty to the leader; not upon qualifications. Not only in Communist countries is that a practice, by the way.

Without forcing Soviet citizens to buy them, most of those 20,000 serge suits are going to rot in the stores.

That is only one way in which the capitalist system is far better than communism or socialism.

I am sure you have heard supposedly learned men say that the early Christians practiced a form of communism. They could not be further wrong. Most Christians in the early churches were generous to a fault and shared what they had with those "less fortunate" than themselves. Does that term, "less fortunate," ring a bell with you? It should—we hear it all the time, when the ones to whom that appellation is applied are sometimes not unfortunate at all but guilty of depending upon others to take care of them and their families.

Not so much a lack of good fortune as a lack of ambition, initiative and pride.

Karl Marx said, "Religion is the sigh of the oppressed creature, the heart of a heartless world, and the soul of soulless *conditions*. It is the opium of the people." Religion had no place within the communist government or among its people.

Socialism comes in all sizes and designs. Some entail the state ownership of all factories and means of distribution of goods; nearer full-blown communism. Others, while not owning those businesses, heavily regulate what is manufactured and how much the business can charge for their product—even to whom they might sell their products.

What American socialists find so appealing is the health-care systems operated in the European-style socialist states. They point out the fact that, "Health care is free!"

No, neither health care nor much of anything else is free. Somebody has to pay for it.

There is an old story that I once heard the Miami Dolphin's football coach, Don Shula, tell about a king who told his minions to distill all the wisdom in the world for his quick perusal.

After a few months, they came back to him with a three-volume tome. "No, no—I want it smaller." They came back with a single, smaller book. He refused that. A three-page memo? He didn't like that.

At last, one of the men came in bearing a single page of paper, on which were written these words: "There is no such thing as a free lunch."

Taxes in those European socialist countries our Progressive friends so envy are so high that there is little incentive for entrepreneurship. Why start a business and make money if you have to give most of what you make to the government?

Socialism is seductive, though, isn't it? The thought of getting something for nothing is appealing to those who have no ambition to earn more, live better or provide better for their family than did their parents. In socialism, the government picks winners and losers; it makes little difference how talented you are, how great your capacity for work, or how much you contribute to the business for which you work.

Why work? That was a common feeling among communal farmers and laborers in Russia. People were just not that into helping the government that does not pass along the fruits of their labor.

That is something the Soviets discovered when they relented, at the end of three or four failed '5-year plans' for increasing productivity and the amount of foodstuff grown on their collective farms. It was pathetically small, no matter how many threats they made to the workers to get more out of them. Then the collectivists made the mistake of allowing those working the collective fields to cultivate a small individually held garden in front of where they stayed in barrack-style housing. The produce from these small gardens was theirs to consume, or even to sell at a local market. To the Communists shock and amazement, these small plots produced more than the hundreds of acres of the collective farms. It was an eye-opening experience for many. You see, when a man can benefit from his hard work, he will increase his output of labor many fold.

Chapter 22

PROGRESSIVISM

PROGRESSIVISM IS A movement that had its roots in the latter decade of the 19th Century and the early 20th Century. The impetus behind the movement was the fear that the Industrial Revolution had changed dramatically the American workforce, the banking and monetary requirements and to some extent the social structure of our nation. Progressives believed that the Founders' view of the Constitution was outmoded—that it had been drawn up in a very different America, and that it was time to jettison the old Constitution and draw up one that would allow the federal government a larger role in protecting citizens from the ravages of the wealthy corporations. Some cited the supposed concept of positive government that Alexander Hamilton favored had a far greater role in the lives of the people. Progressives believed it needed to be far more proactive in holding the avaricious corporate leaders at bay, and to be more equitable in the division of corporate profits.

While there were more of them, historians agree on the point that the title "Progressive" fit at least three former Presidents: Theodore Roosevelt, William Howard Taft and Woodrow Wilson. Early Progressives fought with conservative judges who were 'strict constructionists' because these men resisted adding to the powers exercised by the government. Progressives wanted the courts to be more protective of the people against social evils; to take the "choke-chain" off and quit limiting the authority of government.

Historian William E. Leuchtenburg, an authority on one of our nation's most active Progressive Presidents, Franklin D. Roosevelt, said that while Roosevelt did not lead America into Socialism or into becoming a welfare state, what Roosevelt's New Deal did accomplish was that it kept capitalism from absolutely collapsing—if just barely. We can agree that capitalism was still alive after FDR died and the reins were relinquished to Vice President Harry S. Truman. What is less certain is that Roosevelt's actions had anything to do with its survival. It certainly never was the same capitalism after the Roosevelt years, but it does still exist. Of the important accomplishments of FDR, for good or for ill, perhaps his most lasting "gift" was that from his time forward, many people looked to the federal government as their savior from almost any problem. That was new for Americans, who had, prior to the Roosevelt administration, believed with the Founders that the best government was a limited government.

One of the problems with which Progressives struggled prior to and during the New Deal era was illegal voting and how it "corrupted" the political system. They opposed what they called "saloon keepers and precinct bosses who stuffed ballots" *and encouraged ineligible people to vote.* To solve these problems, Progressives shut down saloons on election day and adopted restrictions like literacy tests to limit the votes of those too ignorant to understand the issues. Yes, It was Progressives who introduced literacy tests! In southern states, ways were found to disenfranchise black voters, but for a very different reason from those alleged in later years. In the Progressive era, it was believed that *white conservatives* "bought" the votes of the blacks to control elections. It was therefore easier to *disenfranchise the blacks* than to control the wealthy and powerful men who bought their votes.

My, how things have changed!

This is but one of many facts about which one will never hear a Progressive speak the truth.

What a change almost 100 years has brought to American politics! At present, Progressives are bitterly opposed to having every prospective voter present a form of identification before exercising his franchise. They now say that checking IDs at the polling places is a means of suppressing the vote—principally black vote. Wait—was it not for the purpose of preventing wealthy whites from buying African American votes that the Progressives had once sought to disenfranchise blacks?

In any event, since possession of an ID is required for any number of daily activities, it strains credulity to believe that an adult African American in this nation would not possess not one but several cards or documents that would suffice as a means of identification. If you were an African American, would you not feel insulted that the Progressives think you are not intelligent enough or engaged enough to possess an ID? The only downside to quashing the requirement that a prospective voter present a verifiable ID before being permitted to cast his ballot is... that it would provide a paper trail that might preclude a person voting in multiple districts. Is that a bad idea?

The Progressive attitude toward sex is almost surprising, since Friedrich Hegel, an early 19th century German philosopher that Progressives have always much admired, was rather old-fashioned in his views on sexual matters. One would be unable to differentiate his views from those of a modern-day conservative. To get to the mind-set of the Progressive on this point, one must go back to their belief that nothing that limits self-expression (self-realization, as John Dewey called it in the 1890s) can be good, because each man has within himself the knowledge as to what it takes to make him feel fulfilled, and no god has the right to prohibit acts that bring self-realization or self-fulfillment. Ergo, no limitation on sexual activities or proclivities is acceptable. All sexual idiosyncrasies are to be tolerated, even applauded.

One other major departure between the Founders of our nation and the Progressives is with a point of view that we have tried to offer as a means of pulling our great country out of the present morass. You see, the Founders believed that God was both the God of nature and the author of moral and spiritual law by which human beings were to order their lives. Many Progressives, if they recognize God at all, see Him merely as the God of nature; nothing more. Some may identify more closely with the opinion of the afore-mentioned Hegel that "...the State is the divine idea as it exists on earth."

Progressives have pursued a policy of minimizing, even trivializing and almost criminalizing Christians and the Christian God. Prayer in schools has been legally estopped, as has been the former habit of some cities to erect a crèche in the public square at Christmastime—or what Progressives prefer to call "Winter Holiday" or "Xmas." It is a violation of the law in many places to display the Ten Commandments or the Christian flag. Efforts are well underway to stifle the discussion of Christianity—not "religion"; Christianity—in the public marketplace. The belief that many feel is the credo around which our nation's Constitution was constructed is now viewed by Progressives as something wholly offensive to themselves and to others—particularly our Muslim brothers. So it must go. It must be suppressed, marginalized, ridiculed.

Perhaps some of my secular humanist friends can enlighten me: why, if Christianity is so stupid, so simple, so child-like and senseless—why do you spend an inordinate amount of time trying to quash it? Won't it die on its own inability to sustain such idiotic beliefs?

You should have learned in elementary school that you never engage in an argument with an idiot. Why? Because after about five minutes of arguing, onlookers will no longer be able to ascertain which is the idiot. One other observation: One should not disparage a competitor's product while extoling his own. The person you are trying to sell may never have heard of Christianity, but once you mention it, I can almost promise you, he is going to have to find out for himself whether your criticism is valid.

The election of 2020 will go a long way towards establishing whether the Constitution as put together with much consideration, discussion, thought and, yes, earnest prayer will continue to be the law of the land or whether it, too, will be jettisoned in favor of a document to make Socialism the framework for government in America. At least *this once more*, the choice is ours—and here, we are talking about the American citizens. Should the results be those sought by the Progressives, your vote—like those of the Venezuelans for the last 20+ years, will possibly forever be for naught.

Chapter 23

ARE PROGRESSIVES THE PARTY OF THE BITTER, THE PARTNERS OF COMMUNISM?

THERE IS A widely held observation that the Progressives in our country are a bitter bunch of people, many of them seemingly with hearts so full of hatred that there is no room for any other emotion or driving force. You could say without fear of contradiction that a majority of them hate President Donald Trump. There are a goodly number of conservatives who are not all that fond of Mr. Trump, for reasons easily explained. Nevertheless, he is our President, and it is apparent he is trying to keep the promises he made to the American people—which was the basis for his election.

Enough Americans agreed with the program President Trump outlined in his campaign to have elected him to that office. Certainly, the America he visualizes is not compatible with the country his adversaries see as their goal. There appears to be more to the divide than usual, however. The opposing sides see two very different Americas to which they aspire. One group desires a small government and minimal interference by that government in citizens' everyday affairs. As they read the Constitution, that instrument was drafted for the purpose of protecting the citizens from the machination of the government; the fear being that a too-large government will usurp rights not afforded them by the Constitution and will use those purloined "rights" to suppress the protected rights of individual Americans.

The other side largely sees the Constitution as a "living, ever-changing set of rules" that are to be interpreted in light of events and conditions of the present day. President Barack Obama suggested strongly that the Founding Fathers simply did not think of a method for the redistribution of wealth, although he is certain that had they been more fully aware, perhaps a bit more intelligent, they would have added such a clause. No, Mister Obama—I don't think our Founders simply overlooked that "duty".

Both sides, Conservatives and Progressives, swear and attest that they love America, and I'm sure that is true. The question is, *which* America do they love? Which America do YOU love? The one envisioned by the Founders when they drafted the Constitution, or the one wherein many would have the government morph into what the Progressives refer to as "democratic socialism?"

Right now, it appears that all 23 or so candidates of the Democrat party for president favor most or all of the following social programs:

1) Free health care—not only for Americans, but many of the more leftist candidates wish to provide health care for all the immigrants here in our country now—and supposedly for the millions more to come!

2) Free schools, for all the above recipients. That includes free college or university education. All the front-runners, with the possible exception of Joe Biden, favor this.

3) A living wage paid to every person in America, some add "whether he works or not." It is unclear whether the ones who work will get more than the non-workers.

4) Green fuel initiative; some opposing jet aircraft and flatulent cows, among other things—estimated to cost 2.5 trillion dollars a year. Considering that the entire 2018 budget is $4.5 trillion, that figure would represent an increase of more than half again the 2018 budget.

How do we pay for it?

5) Tax corporations and the rich.

Let us look at a person whose influence in Progressive circles continues to this day, though he has been dead since 1972.

Some of you may not be familiar with Saul Alinsky, credited with being America's first Community Organizer. Alinsky wrote a couple of books, among them *Rules for Radicals*. He had his own ideas as to what the political makeup of America should be, and he tried to outline a way that the liberal/progressives of this nation might create a social (Socialist) state.

Here is how to create a social state, in the opinion of Saul Alinsky:

> *There are 8 levels of control that must be obtained before you are able to create a social state.*
>
> *The first is the most important.*
>
> *1) Healthcare — Control healthcare and you control the people*
>
> *2) Poverty — Increase the Poverty level as high as possible, poor people are easier to control and will not fight back if you are providing everything for them to live.*

3) *Debt — Increase the debt to an unsustainable level. That way you are able to increase taxes, and this will produce more poverty.*

4) *Gun Control — Remove the ability to defend themselves **from the Government**. That way you are able to create a police state.*

5) *Welfare — Take control of every aspect of their lives (Food, Housing, and Income).*

6) *Education — Take control of what people read and listen to — take control of what children learn in school.*

7) *Religion — Remove the belief in God from the Government and schools.*

8) *Class Warfare — Divide the people into the wealthy and the poor. This will cause more discontent and it will be easier to take (Tax) the wealthy with the support of the poor.*

If you believe that our former President, Barack Obama, did a creditable job of advancing all the above goals in his eight years in that office, do not allow me to disabuse you of that idea. Remember, as far as Obama allowed history to record, the only job he ever held outside politics was as a Community Organizer.

Let's look at the accomplishments attained by Obama and his administration:

1) Healthcare: Persuaded the Progressives in Congress to pass the Affordable Healthcare Act, or Obamacare as it became known. Not a single Republican voted for that failed measure.

2) Poverty: There were 34 million citizens receiving food stamps before 2008. That number increased by more than

35 percent to 47 million during Obama's administration. Average income for most Americans dropped more than an average of $2,500 and 50,000,000 citizens lived below poverty level.

3) Debt: The National debt more than doubled under Obama's leadership, from 9 trillion to more than 20 trillion—more debt in eight years than all the previous administrations combined.

4) Gun Control: Here the Obama administration and Progressive congressmen tried very hard but succeeded in only minor restrictions in gun ownership.

5) Welfare: Federal non-discretionary spending (entitlements, like welfare, etc.) increased from 19.6 percent of GDP in 2007 to 23.6 percent in 2010. Obama asked for $10.3 billion for the next 10 years, or $250,000 for each person, $1,000,000 for each family in poverty. Largest welfare percentage ever.

6) Education: America spends $15,171 per student on education. Switzerland spends $14,922; Mexico spends $2,993. U.S. 4th graders were 11th in Math skills in 2010, and 15-year-old Americans were 31st in math literacy, 23rd in science among developed nations. We do an excellent job in boosting our children's self-esteem; little in giving them reason for genuine pride in accomplishments.

7) Religion: The influence the Church and church leaders once had in American society has waned dramatically. We have accepted the Progressive idea that the First Amendment provides a separation between church and state that precludes any discussion of God in the public marketplace. Secular humanists are carrying the day when it comes to their success in driving any mention of Jesus Christ out of

any public discourse. Shame of us as Christians for accepting that situation.

8) Class Warfare: I believe this nation is more divided today than at any time since the Civil War. Progressives have concluded that any disagreement with their views has to be based on one of the following: sexism, racism, homophobia, xenophobia, ethnocentrism, or some other phobia yet to be defined. They disallow the possibility that a conservative might hold an honest opinion in opposition to their own ideas. They teach that conservatives deliberately starve poor people and those citizens of color. What is the hope for a civil discourse? Sadly, just now, there is none.

You may be aware that Hillary Rodham, before she became Hillary Rodham Clinton, wrote her master's thesis at Wellesley College... on Saul Alinsky and his *Rules for Radicals*. She has long been an admirer.

By the way, why do you suppose the Democrat/Progressives are so determined to get a single-payer health care program, controlled by the government? Look back to Alinsky's number one and most important goal for the establishment of a Socialist state. Rule number six is...

Education – Take control of what people read and listen to; take control of what children learn in school.

One would have to read Saul's book to understand for himself what Alinsky meant by that statement. Suffice to say he had little interest in enumerating the accomplishments of George Washington or any of the other Founding Fathers. While he was not proven to be a Communist, Alinsky once said he would work with anyone to achieve his goals. By the way, his book was dedicated to Lucifer—Satan. To some, that might be a recommendation, but to others...

Community Organizer in Chicago is the only real job Barack Obama ever had before being elected to the Congress of Illinois. Where did he receive training for such a demanding job, and what does he plan to do with that education?

Obama Aims to Train 'Next Generation' of Anti-Trump Activists

> "Most prominently we're gonna be interested in fig-uring out how we can develop the next generation of leaders. [we will] be trying to create a platform where young activists ... can get trained and learn from each other."

Obama repeated the criticism personalities like NFL quarter-back Colin Kaepernick and his refusal to stand for the national anthem and demonstrations in Ferguson in opposition to police brutality. Both, he said, called attention to a real problem without proposing any real solution.

Alluding to Martin Luther King Jr. and Democrat Representative from Georgia John Lewis, the former president said that both, "would begin with the protest but then very rapidly engage in the powers that be to say, 'We will stop protesting when you use this specific thing.'" Barack Obama picked an appearance at a *town-hall meeting broadcast by ESPN(?) *to announce Michelle and his current project. Some will see this as nothing more than good PR for Obama's foundation in Chicago, while it is more likely we are seeing his return to his community organizing days he learned from Saul Alinsky and his leftist disciples.

During the town hall. Obama said he wants to create a "platform" to train the next generation of activists and leaders.

The specific things that Obama is thinking of are what gives many a reason to pause.

Conservative columnist Paul Sperry wrote a commentary for the New York Post over a year ago with the headline, "How Obama is Scheming to Sabotage Trump's Presidency." The 'how' is now becoming more clear.

Sperry described Organize for Action (OFA) then as a "little known but well-funded protesting arm" formed by Obama supporters to recruit leftist protesters. He speculated that Obama was "working behind the scenes to set up what will effectively be a shadow government" to oppose Trump. He wrote:

"Since Donald Trump's election, this little-known but well-funded protesting arm has beefed up staff and ramped up recruitment of young liberal activists, declaring on its website, 'We're not backing down.' Determined to salvage Obama's legacy, it's drawing battle lines on immigration, ObamaCare, race relations and climate change.

Obama is intimately involved in OFA operations and even tweets from the group's <u>account</u>. In fact, he gave marching orders to OFA foot soldiers following Trump's upset victory."

Obama's website links to OFA's that has an extensive network of volunteers. The organization mission statement is that it exists to "rear the next generation of progressive grassroots organizers."

Byron York of the National Review warned before Obama's first run for president in 2008 that the then little-known freshman senator had an insatiable <u>hunger</u> for <u>change</u> and power.

York contended then that one can only understand where Barack Obama might go by understanding from whence he came. In other words, read Saul Alinsky book Rules for Radicals and you will find the blueprint that brought Obama to power and the reason he will never follow many past president's pattern of fading from public attention or <u>serve</u> as a senior statesman when needed.

In Rules for Radicals Alinsky encouraged a young Obama community organizer to be "an abrasive agent to rub raw the resentments of the people of the community; to fan latent hostilities of many of the people to the point of overt expressions."

York explains, " Once such hostilities were 'whipped up to a fighting pitch'... he steered his group toward <u>confrontation,</u> in the form of picketing, demonstrating, and general hell-raising...At first, the organizer tackled small stuff... later, when the group gained confidence, the organizer could take on bigger targets. But at all times, the organizer's goal was not to lead his people anywhere but to encourage them to take action on their own behalf."

Instead of war in the streets, Obama now leads a far different kind of social justice army than his early Chicago days, but his goal is what it has always been – instigate a movement that gives him power so he can move on to a bigger cause and gain more power.

Listening to Barack Obama leaves no doubt what he sees as his next path to power. He wants to train an army of "community organizers"

*made in his image to combat conservatives in America and more spe-
cifically President Trump's agenda.*

~ *American Liberty Report*

***This was billed as a 'conference of the Undefeateds', sponsored by
ESPN and held at North Carolina A & T University, Greensboro,
North Carolina on October 16, 2016. Hosted and moderated by
SportsCenter anchor Stan Verrett, _An Undefeated Conversation
with President Obama: Sports, Race and Achievement_ aired at
10 p.m. EST.**

There is something else that might be instructive to read and
take note of.

You are about to read a list of 45 goals that found their way
down the halls of our great Capitol back in 1963. As you read this,
39 + years later, you should be shocked by the events that have
played themselves out. These goals originally appeared in *The Naked
Communist* by W. Cleon Skousen (another retired FBI Agent) and
were printed out and made a part of the Library of Congress.

Are any of these Communist goals reflected in some of the policies our own country has pursued in the past? You must honestly
answer that question.

1) U.S. acceptance of coexistence as the only alternative to
   atomic war. ALMOST THERE
2) U.S. willingness to capitulate in preference to engaging in
   atomic war. ALMOST THERE
3) Develop the illusion that total disarmament [by] the
   United States would be a demonstration of moral
   strength. WAVERING.

4) Permit free trade between all nations regardless of Communist affiliation and regardless of whether or not items could be used for war. ALMOST THERE.

5) Extension of long-term loans to Russia and Soviet satellites. N/A NOW.

6) Provide American aid to all nations regardless of Communist domination. DONE.

7) Grant recognition of Red China. Admission of Red China to the U.N. – DONE.

8) Set up East and West Germany as separate states in spite of Khrushchev's promise in 1955 to settle the German question by free elections under supervision of the U.N. – UN-DONE. Ended with the tearing down of the Berlin Wall in 1991.

9) Prolong the conferences to ban atomic tests because the United States has agreed to suspend tests as long as negotiations are in progress. – DONE

10) Allow all Soviet satellites individual representation in the U.N. DONE

11) Promote the U.N. as the only hope for mankind. If its charter is rewritten, demand that it be set up as a one-world government with its own independent armed forces. (Some Communist leaders believe the world can be taken over as easily by the U.N. as by Moscow. Sometimes these two centers compete with each other as they are now doing in the Congo.)–DONE

12) Resist any attempt to outlaw the Communist Party. – HAPPENING EVERY DAY.

13) Do away with all loyalty oaths. ALMOST THERE. — THEY MEAN VERY LITTLE.

14) Continue giving Russia access to the U.S. Patent Office.–?

15) Capture one or both of the political parties in the United States.–???? HAS THIS BEEN DONE? SOME WOULD SAY IT HAS BEEN ACCOMPLISHED.

16) Use technical decisions of the courts to weaken basic American institutions by claiming their activities violate civil rights. – DONE

17) Get control of the schools. Use them as transmission belts for socialism and current Communist propaganda. Soften the curriculum. Get control of teachers' associations. WHAT DO YOU THINK? Put the party line in text-books.–ALMOST DONE

18) Gain control of all student newspapers.–???? WHAT DO YOU THINK?

19) Use student riots to foment public protests against programs or organizations which are under Communist attack. – DONE AND DOING

20) Infiltrate the press. Get control of book-review assignments, editorial writing, policy-making positions.–???? DO YOU STILL QUESTION THIS?

21) Gain control of key positions in radio, TV, and motion pictures.–???? SEE ABOVE.

22) Continue discrediting American culture by degrading all forms of artistic expression. An American Communist cell was told to "eliminate all good sculpture from parks and buildings, substitute shapeless, awkward and meaningless forms." – DONE AND DOING

23) Control art critics and directors of art museums. "Our plan is to promote ugliness, repulsive, meaningless art."–DONE AND CONTINUING

24) Eliminate all laws governing obscenity by calling them "censorship" and a violation of free speech and free press. – DONE

25) Break down cultural standards of morality by promoting pornography and obscenity in books, magazines, motion pictures, radio, and TV. – DONE

26) Present homosexuality, degeneracy and promiscuity as "normal, natural, healthy." – DONE

27) Infiltrate the churches and replace revealed religion with "social" religion. Discredit the Bible and emphasize the need for intellectual maturity, which does not need a "religious crutch." – DONE AND CONTINUING

28) Eliminate prayer or any phase of religious expression in the schools on the ground that it violates the principle of "separation of church and state." – DONE

29) Discredit the American Constitution by calling it inadequate, old-fashioned, out of step with modern needs, a hindrance to cooperation between nations on a worldwide basis. – DONE AND CONTINUING

30) Discredit the American Founding Fathers. Present them as selfish aristocrats who had no concern for the "common man." – DONE

31) Belittle all forms of American culture and discourage the teaching of American history on the ground that it was only a minor part of the "big picture." Give more emphasis to Russian history since the Communists took over. – DONE

32) Support any socialist movement to give centralized control over any part of the culture—education, social agencies, welfare programs, mental health clinics, etc. – CONTINUING

33) Eliminate all laws or procedures which interfere with the operation of the Communist apparatus. – DONE

34) Eliminate the House Committee on Un-American Activities. – DONE

35) Discredit and eventually dismantle the FBI. – IN THE PROCESS

36) Infiltrate and gain control of more unions. — WANING

37) Infiltrate and gain control of big business. – SUCCESS

38) Transfer some of the powers of arrest from the police to social agencies. Treat all behavioral problems as psychiatric disorders which no one but psychiatrists can understand [or treat]. -DONE

39) Dominate the psychiatric profession and use mental health laws as a means of gaining coercive control over those who oppose Communist goals. – DONE

40) Discredit the family as an institution. Encourage promiscuity and easy divorce. – DONE AND DOING

41) Emphasize the need to raise children away from the negative influence of parents. Attribute prejudices, mental blocks and retarding of children to suppressive influence of parents. — CONTINUING

42) Create the impression that violence and insurrection are legitimate aspects of the American tradition; that students and special-interest groups should rise up and use "united force" to solve economic, political or social problems. — DONE

43) Overthrow all colonial governments before native populations are ready for self-government. — DONE.

44) Internationalize the Panama Canal. – DONE

45) Repeal the Connally reservation so the United States cannot prevent the World Court from seizing jurisdiction [over domestic problems. Give the World Court jurisdiction] over nations and individuals alike. — BEING ATTEMPTED EVERY DAY.

Many of the items in the 45 points that the Communists wish to achieve in America are being promoted in college classrooms all across our land. One must ask, "Who is stirring up student violence against properly elected leaders?" Which party or group stands to profit from these efforts? Or are these ANTIFA raids and disturbances, made in an effort to intimidate conservative politicians and conservative voters, truly spontaneous? If you believe that, perhaps you should also check into the sale of beachfront property in Arizona.

"Useful Idiots" is a pejorative term that was used, not by J. Edgar Hoover but by the Russians themselves to describe Soviet sympathizers in Western countries, and in the United States in particular. It is thought that Soviet leader Lenin was the first to use the term and it was used by the Soviets for many years to ridicule misguided Americans who were willing to take the Soviet/Marxist side against their own country.

"Oh," you might say. "Those 45 points were made long ago—before Glasnost; before Khrushchev and the collapse of the Soviet Union and the reorganization of the new Russia."

Russian attempts to interfere in our elections and their alliance, in direct opposition to America, with that terrible despot Assad to suppress most violently the desire for freedom on the part of Syrian citizens would not seem to be acts indicative of a desire to practice *laissez-faire* when it comes to America. It can easily be established that the current Russian Prime Minister, Vladimir Putin, desires above all things to re-establish Russia as one of the most powerful nations on the earth; to recapture the halcyon days of the USSR. That hardly sounds like a formula for leaving America to follow its own chosen course of action. America must wane in strength and influence before Russia can be a dominant force again.

No, Russia is not a friend or ally of America—*as it (America) is currently constituted.*

Russia is not continually exerting efforts to insinuate Communist ideals and practices into America, or any other country, out of "friendship." Russia's end goal is to establish complete hegemony over as much of the world as they can manage. That has been their goal since the Bolshevik Revolution of 1917 and continues to be the aim of the Communist Russian nation to this day.

It isn't just that the Progressives want all those things in the New America. It is that they absolutely reject any idea of paring back their list. If conservatives don't agree with their plans *in toto*, then they are suffering from hatred based on racism, sexism, homophobia, xenophobia, misogyny or some other fear or hatred to be named later.

Progressives literally have no patience with or tolerance for those who disagree with their view regarding what is best for the country. Worse, those who do not see things their way are not just mistaken, they are stupid, dumb, backward, evil, intent upon killing off blacks, Hispanics, old people, women, homosexuals—have we left out anyone?

Why does the media—why do we, the end-users of what must pass for "news" nowadays—put up with such obvious hogwash? To call such language exaggeration is to dignify it. What is the purpose of such hyperbole? It is the furthest thing from trying to identify what are real problems in America. It is to demonize a group that, according to the results of the 2016 elections, amounts to about fifty percent of our population. If fifty percent of our population is comprised of stupid, evil, homophobic killers, is there even a glimmer of hope that anyone in the other fifty percent may survive the coming onslaught?

To refer to the language many Progressives use to describe their opponents as "hyperbole" is to give that verbiage a modicum of respect it does not deserve. Language like that should never be dignified in any manner. It should be entirely rejected as unworthy of utterance by anyone with an I Q north of sixty. Indeed, parents should be ashamed of their first grader who would use such silly phrases as those written or uttered unapologetically by supposedly respected leaders of the media and of the Progressive party—or is that a redundancy?

That being so, and I firmly believe that it is, does that alter your estimation of the intellect of those individuals? It should.

SECTION IV

The Way Back

Chapter 24

CHANGING GEARS

THIS BOOK HAS attempted to point out several important events that revealed a slackening in our nation's resolve to do the right, the proper thing—with our own people but particularly in our dealings with other countries. There was a concomitant creeping tolerance for first naughty and then egregious acts of disgusting behaviors that would have shocked our grandparents.

Theodore Dalrymple wrote a book entitled Life At the Bottom (published in Great Britain in November of 2011 by Rowman and Littlefield) in which he castigated the British intelligentsia for excusing the criminal acts of young, mostly white, British hooligans. Thomas Sowell, in his book Intellectuals and Race writes on page 123 that the intelligentsia on both sides of the ocean preach " . . . a social vision that excuses barbarism by blaming society, thus allowing the intelligentsia to align themselves with the angels against the forces of evil." Sowell laments the fact that while he gets excoriated for writing about the barbarism of American blacks, Dalrymple gets away with his criticisms because the British intelligentsia cannot accuse him of racism. Intellectuals and Race by Thomas Sowell, Barnes and Noble, March 12, 2013.

What becomes obvious when one takes an elongated look at our national history is that there have been times when our country had reason to be united—particularly in World Wars, depressions, etc. During those periods, church attendance was higher, demonstrations of patriotism flourished and were clearly heart-felt. People seemed to have the sense that we're all in this together and worked in concert to get the problem resolved.

That all began to change in the fifties, and greatly accelerated in the sixties. The group that was referred to generally as "hippies" in that era seemed to reject all things heretofore seen as more-or-less sacrosanct. They seemed to say, "Whatever my father was for, I am dead set against." Since many of these rebellious youngsters had grown up as members of a church of some kind, perhaps there was a reluctance to make a complete break with their spiritual roots. Rather than attending church services, however, this group took a different attitude to all things spiritual; initially asserting that spiritual matters were not all that important, then gradually having less and less regard for God and the Bible until in the present day, their mantra seems to be that anyone who believes in Jesus Christ is a downright fool.

There is the chance that the present concern with COVID-19 has reminded us of our mortality. We have been reminded just how tenuous is our hold on life. Perhaps this is a good time to reflect upon the past and recall how very much we need each other in perilous times like these. It is a good time to deliberate the differences that have kept us separated for the past twenty to thirty years and have made enemies of people with whom we formerly shared a collegial friendship. Reflecting upon the brevity of life, we must look at how the few years allocated to us on earth could be spent in harmony and concern for each other, rather than being divided by hatred and resentment.

There is a road map already laid out for us to follow to achieve that consonance. It was outlined for us by our Founding Fathers in an instrument called The Constitution for the United States of America—emphasis on *united*.

The Founders provided liberties and freedoms for the citizens of this new nation that no other country had ever enjoyed. They deliberated upon these freedoms, debating how Americans would handle them, but concluded that since this was a nation with firm roots in the Judeo-Christian ethos, the love and concern for others built into that religious heritage would be sufficient to keep the country on that path. Indeed, it did last for more than two-hundred years before the influence of religion diminished, and an acceptance of or tolerance for greed and avarice encouraged mercenary citizens to put all emphasis on their own rights, and consider little or not at all the responsibilities that must accompany the exercise of these rights.

A democratic republic cannot survive in such an atmosphere.

Does a majority in America desire to remain a democratic republic?

If the answer is affirmative, is there a solution to the problems that currently beset our society and civilization?

Yes, there is a solution . . .

Chapter 25

RECOVERING LOST VALUES

Keep your thoughts positive, because your thoughts become your words.
Keep your words positive, because your words become your behavior
Keep your behavior positive, because your behavior becomes your habit.
Keep your habits positive, because your habits become your values.
Keep your values positive, because your values become your destiny.
-Mahatma Ghandi

National Character

IN 2015, TOWNHALL Magazine posted the below article by D.W. Wilber, a counterterrorism analyst and former CIA officer. It ran under the headline "A Matter of Our National Character."

> During last week's Republican presidential debate, the former CEO of Hewlett Packard and Republican candidate Carly Fiorina made an impassioned comment about the Planned Parenthood

abortion for profit scandal, stating that it was a matter of our national character.

Indeed Ms. Fiorina was correct, Americans cannot stand by and simply ignore the fact that Planned Parenthood has been butchering tiny babies and selling their body parts for a hefty profit for quite some time now. Any country that would advocate for that practice to continue needs to do some serious self-evaluation about what kind of a people we are.

Also considering the recent reports coming out of the Pentagon saying that American soldiers in Afghanistan are being told to "look the other way" when Afghan military and police colleagues sexually abuse young boys, that too calls into question what is America's character.

American soldiers with otherwise stellar records are being punished and forced out of the military because they have exhibited what are the very best qualities of American character in Afghanistan, for refusing to stand by and look the other way when young children are being sexually abused and exploited.

During the Vietnam War, American helicopter pilot Hugh Thompson refused to do nothing when he saw atrocities being committed by American troops under the command of Lieutenant William Calley in the South Vietnamese hamlet of My Lai.

He took decisive action to prevent further loss of innocent life. Truly an example of what the character of the American military is all about.

But how far have we fallen as a nation when we are willing to accept Planned Parenthood's depravity, with pro-abortion politicians making excuses for Planned Parenthood, and even refusing to watch video-taped evidence clearly showing that the sales of unborn children's body parts was encouraged by Planned Parenthood policymakers? Does the "head-in-the-sand" tactic change the facts? Hardly.

How far have we fallen as a nation where our military leadership is instructing soldiers to turn a blind eye to atrocities committed in war and not protecting the most vulnerable among us, instead of following the example of Hugh Thompson?

For more than 60 years now we have watched as American culture has coarsened to the point where what was once considered deviant behavior has been "mainstreamed" by politicians concerned only with courting a particular voting bloc.

Drug usage has become commonplace, in fact even legalized in some states to facilitate a drug culture concerned only with getting high. Ask any of them about what President John F. Kennedy once called on Americans to do, to "ask not what your country can do for you, but ask what you can do for your country," and you'll be met with a glazed over blank stare. Those sentiments expressed by President Kennedy are foreign to the "if it feels good do it" class in this country.

Daily it seems Americans are subjected to examples of the downward spiral this country has embarked upon, which eventually will lead to a complete societal breakdown. Anyone who promotes what had once been considered to be "mainstream family values" are shouted down by the liberal left and called "haters."

The character of our nation has gotten out of whack. Common decency, moral character, and conservative thought are ridiculed by the proponents of modern culture among the Hollywood elites who promote through their films and programming something far different than "traditional values." Traditional values appear to be nothing more than a punchline out on the "left coast."

In Washington, D.C. Americans are forced to vote for the "lesser of two evils" repeatedly in elections where politicians tell us all that they are going to do for us, when they have no intentions of doing so once elected.

In the Halls of Congress, it seems one has to go along to get along. Any outsider who speaks to principle and integrity is hounded out of office by the political powerbrokers and career politicians occupying the positions of leadership.

And in the White House lies and illegal actions have become a daily occurrence with an administration thumbing their collective noses at "we the people." Caring little for what the majority of Americans have voiced and responding only to a minority who demand more and more changes to American culture.

Like an old analog television our moral character as a nation seems to be on the fritz. We are now living in an era where what was once right is now wrong, and what was wrong is now right. And our character as a nation suffers.

Let it be clear that the writer was referring to the administration of Barack Obama—not that of Donald Trump.

Indeed, it was the Obama administration whose rules made it impossible for an American soldier to confront an Afghani military or police officer committing a crime in his presence.

Consider what happened to an Army Green Beret soldier who confronted an Afghan Police Commander he had helped train. That man raped a 12-year-old boy and then beat up the boy's mother because she turned him in to the Americans.

"It's sad to think that a child rapist is put above one of our elite military operators. Sergeant Martland was left with no other choice but to intervene in a bad situation. ... The Army should stand up for what's right and should not side with a corrupt Afghan police officer," Hunter told Fox News.

The Hunter quoted in the article was California Representative Duncan Hunter.

> *Sgt. 1st Class Charles Martland found out that he was to be booted out of service, a casualty of the Army's Qualitative Management Program, an involuntary separation measure for soldiers with black marks on their records. Since then, the soldier has been fighting to remain in the Army.*

> *The Army Board for Correction of Military Records reviewed Martland's case and decided to remove the soldier from the QMP list, confirmed Army spokesman Lt. Col. Jerry Pionk in an emailed statement. The board's action "will allow him to remain in the Army," Pionk said.*

Is it possible for a nation to have a "character," in the sense that a majority, or at least an influential minority may possess certain qualities of decency and probity that guide not only their personal decisions, but heavily impact the direction a country might follow?

For instance, would you say about Iran that this is a country desirous of living in peace with neighbors, earnest in their quest for harmony in the Middle East, and always willing to assist other nations in establishing a democratic form of government?

No?

The truth is, the character of Iran is almost the exact opposite of the national character described above. But do they have a "national character?" I believe they do.

America has a national character as well, although it is in the process of being challenged as never before. Perhaps "challenged" is not the correct word. No, there is and has been for more than sixty years a concentrated effort to completely overhaul and reject all those beliefs we have entertained about ourselves since we became a nation. It is not so much that those involved in this struggle have a definite goal towards which they are striving. It is more a total disaffection with what America has always stood for and has been. Unsure of what they wish to change our national character to, they nonetheless desire wholeheartedly to destroy the America afforded us by the Founding Fathers.

You will recall that the second part of Alexis de Tocqueville's addendum (as it is apparently erroneously recorded) was, "When she (America) ceases to be good, she will cease to be great."

Has America "ceased to be good?" If she has, or if some of the bloom is off the original experience with goodness as a factor in good government, when did that patina of goodness begin to grow dim, and what caused it?

It is the goodness that enabled Americans to be great. Certainly, Americans were an ambitious people. There was not, however, the wide-spread acceptance of avarice that would seek one's own advancement at the expense of others. The influence that good people had on each other served as a deterrent to bad behavior. Few people wanted to be seen as the sort of Simon Legree (from *Uncle Tom's Cabin*) who would take advantage of the ill fortune of his neighbor to advance his own wealth. There were enough mean and inconsiderate people in every village to make themselves noticeable, but the fact was, they were easily identifiable by their absence of concern for others, and their influence on the community proper was at best minimal.

In this, Tocqueville seems to be in harmony with views held by Alexander Hamilton and many other patriotic Americans who were nevertheless skeptical that man would continue to abide by the Christian "Golden Rule"—to "Do unto others as you would have them do unto you" into the distant future. He did believe, as did Hamilton and others, that with all the freedoms and liberties afforded the American people by their Constitution, it would not be long before some among them would be taking advantage of those freedoms and depriving others of theirs.

There are several matters, formerly handled with relative ease by children and families that now appear to be almost insoluble problems. For instance:

Bullying

If you were to tune into a television talk show today, you might believe that a new phenomenon has appeared over the past few years on the societal scene in America. It is called "bullying." Ever heard of it? Some guests on these shows insist that bullying is a huge problem, and that the law must deal with it—or school administrators must make protecting their children from bullying a top priority. It is a matter of life or death. This crude behavior threatens the very lives of our children, and it must be stopped immediately.

I do not wish to minimize the effect on children of egregious bullying, and whole-heartedly agree that effective measures be adopted to stop that kind of treatment immediately. However, many parents are unwilling to allow their sons and daughters to learn for themselves how to deal with the run-of-the-mill bully. Believing themselves to be the very epitome of good parents, they intervene on behalf of their child, enlisting the assistance of school officials and the police to have the bullying stopped and the bully punished. Sounds good so far, doesn't it?

Only it isn't. What we have done is develop a few generations of people many of whom refuse to act in their own behalf, indeed do not believe that they *can* fend for themselves. How would they know? They have never been given the opportunity to test themselves. They can say, *I don't have to face this problem—Mom will handle it for me.* He/she was right almost every time; Mom or Dad *would* handle it. Made Mom, and maybe even Dad, feel great. Made the child feel good—temporarily. Was what Mom or Dad did a solution to the problem, or was it a Band-Aid placed over a sore that will not, cannot heal without the child having a little skin in the game (pardon that pun)?

This kind of parenting has produced the generation of "snowflakes" that populate our college campuses nationwide.

As long as you are never confronted with a situation that you must handle or suffer dire consequences—even death—being a snowflake has few serious drawbacks. Where are you likely to be able to avoid any sort of aggressive confrontation other than on a college campus?

If you think the possibility of a snowflake succumbing to death rather than defending himself is an exaggeration, perhaps you should get out in the real world more. In that sphere, there are occasions, perhaps rare but nonetheless real, when an individual must fight to defend himself, his family and friends, or his country. Would you have confidence in a military or police force staffed with snowflakes; men and women who have never had to fight for anything in their entire lives to defend your personal and national freedoms?

By now, you are surely asking yourself, "Is he going somewhere with this line of reasoning?"

What began as a rather natural instinct in a parent to wish more for his child than he had been given turned into the creation of a society that has rejected many of the customs, mores and ways of thinking about the world and individual futures that had held for centuries. The child only grows up when he learns to take care of his own problems.

Responsibility

In the '30s, '40s and on into the '50s, children in much of America had little adult supervision of how they spent their leisure time. It is true that children in small towns and rural areas had relatively little free time to begin with, but what time off they had from work and chores, they were often totally on their own, from sunup to sundown. They did have responsibilities to take care of, but once their jobs had been performed, they could take off without telling Mother exactly where they were going or when she might expect them home. If that sounds a little like child neglect to you, you must appreciate that in that era there was undoubtedly less mischief for a child to get into. Use and misuse of alcohol was rampant in many locales, but until sometime in the '60s, drugs—even marijuana—were unheard of in many areas of the United States.

Most parents, in their heart of hearts, knew that their children were going to be confronted with problems, temptations and dangers; that was just a part of life. Most had spoken with their progeny about what to expect and how to handle the problems they might face. Parents in that era believed in their children for the most part or knew not to believe in them. At least, they believed they knew how far they could trust them and how well their defense against the temptation to do something wrong functioned. They also knew if the child got into a jam, he had darn well better be able to get himself out of it, because Mom and Dad were not as near as their cell phone, which had not been invented in that era.

This was also that strange period of time during which if a young man got in trouble at school and got a paddling (yes, corporal punishment was permitted in those days), he could expect another whipping when he got home. The parent invariably took the part of the teacher and did not necessarily believe the protestations of the wayward son. There were exceptions, of course, but that was the general rule. The same expectations extended to that child's dealings with other children. It was assumed that unless it was a particularly intractable problem beyond his ability to deal with it, the child was expected to handle the problem himself. That was healthy, reasonable and good for the child. Many of our most intractable problems had their genesis in the late '50s and early '60s when American parents, for several reasons, decided that their children were not going to be faced with the woes and difficulties their parents had to deal with.

Parents, tracing back to that era of societal upheaval, wanted for their children a happier, more carefree childhood than they had enjoyed. Because, in the mind of the parents, their father and mother had given them next to nothing, they were not going to deprive their child (or children) of any of the "good things of life." Have you ever heard anyone say, "No matter what I asked for as a child, the first word out of my father's mouth was, 'no'!" Somehow, the depth of our deprivation as children grows as we age—along with the distance we had to walk to school in knee-deep snow, with no shoes. You remember that it was five miles to school, and that it was inexplicably uphill both ways. Oh, things were tough!! Sure, we wish more for our children than our parents were capable of giving us. We forget, however, that the most valuable things that we withhold from our children are often time and attention; worth infinitely more than anything that money can buy.

While working so hard to see that our children have "things," and ensuring that they never have to face any physical or emotional hardship, we have insulated them from an important part of character: Responsibility.

One of the more accurate and valuable yardsticks by which we measure maturity and self-worth is how well we accept responsibility for our own actions and how well we demonstrate that maturity to our family and friends. Responsible adults, when confronted with an error they have made or an instance wherein they have behaved badly, do not look for someone else to blame for that lapse. They not only accept responsibility for their actions but expect and accept appropriate punishment for those actions. It is hard to see how a parent who loves his/her child would deny him/her the privilege of becoming a responsible adult. Yet, parents are far too often stunting the mental and emotional growth of their children, turning them into helpless snowflakes.

Discipline

Perhaps one of the most important characteristics or attributes of a citizen of a Democratic Republic is the discipline to restrain one's self and the excesses of those who appear unable to keep their own appetites under control. What is discipline, is it really vital to a civilized society, and how can we best achieve it?

There are essentially two types of discipline—one designed to be succeeded by the other. First, there is the discipline imposed by our parents, then teachers, coaches and others. Only for the more recalcitrant or those who have no or inadequate parental supervision is it necessary for that discipline to be administered by the police and the judicial system. The latter form need not be really limiting; some youngsters have one encounter with the law from the perspective of the lawbreaker and that is enough to convince them that this is no life for anybody to live.

I knew a young man from my hometown who was nineteen years of age and knew everything. He had become so much smarter than his parents that he must have been insufferable to them. The same would be true for anyone else for whom he might have worked or with whom he had any relationship. He was the typical angry young man, although had you asked him the reason for his anger, he would have been hard pressed to tell you what he had to be mad about. His was a small eastern Oklahoma town with maybe ten or twelve old grouches but 2,000 of the best people in the world. It was a wonderful place to grow up; the teachers and other adults in that town treated this young man far better than he deserved. Members of that great church in which he grew up somehow seemed to have more confidence in him than he could muster in his own behalf. It is hard to imagine what would have happened to that hard-headed young man but for the wonderful people of that small town.

At the age of nineteen, this recalcitrant youth unaccountably decided to visit his local Selective Service Draft Board and volunteer for the military draft. For our younger readers, during the '40s, '50s, '60s and on into the '70s young men, upon their 18th birthday, had to register for the Selective Service System "draft." It was sort of a lottery system, but when your name came up, rather than winning a vast sum of money you were inducted into one or the other branches of the armed forces—usually the U. S. Army. The motivation for volunteering for the draft was that if you were drafted, your sentence; er, enlistment, was for two years. I think at that time, an enlistment in the Air Force was for four years, and the Navy wanted three—maybe four. I am sure the Marine enlistment was four years. Anyway, this young man chose the shorter term and selected the Army.

It took only a part of the first day of his enlistment to learn that a non-commissioned officer (Sergeant or Corporal) who had perhaps dropped out of high school—even elementary school!—and might not be the sharpest knife in *any* drawer could tell that draftee what to do, and he had darned well better do it!

Maddening! He was sure he was smarter the day he was born than that non-com was now, and what right did that guy have to tell him what to do? Turns out, his right was appended to his sleeve. He was a Corporal with two stripes or a Sergeant., with three or more stripes, and the draftee was a "slick-sleeve"—nothing. Private

E-1—it doesn't get any lower than that. Any Sgt. or Corporal could have that E-1 doing push-ups all day, sweeping out the barracks at night, and could place him permanently on K P (Kitchen Police) or Guard Duty.

Want to complain? Go see the Chaplain.

Our young man never did that, and neither did anyone else in his thinking mind. The Chaplain would have told him to suck it up and behave like a man.

Now, "wisdom" didn't come to him in a sudden epiphany. It was more like a false dawn on a sleepy summer day that is usually followed by it getting a little darker before the sun finally peeks up over the mountain, a small sliver of orange glow. While a sunrise only takes a matter of minutes, it took our young soldier weeks to gradually become aware that his real enemy was not Sgt. Ramirez, Sgt. Vilosovich, or Corporal White. For him to get along better in the military, something had to change, and it began to dawn on him that the thing that had to reform was... HIMSELF! Rather than waiting to be instructed for the second or third time to do something, he might do it the first time he was asked. Even better, he might anticipate what needed to be done and do it without having to be asked. The beginning of wisdom! The change was dramatic. He not only got along better with the training cadre of his company, but his attitude toward the Army and life in general began to improve.

This was the beginning of that second kind of discipline of which we spoke earlier: Self-discipline.

Do these kinds of disciplines work on everyone? Sadly, no, they do not. Some in school were simply incorrigible and had to be expelled, with no appeal or recourse. Some in the Army had to be given Bad Conduct discharges for their constant infractions against military discipline. For those who did not fight or go AWOL or do any of those things which might earn them a BCD but who were constantly in minor scrapes, usually the result of trying to get out of performing their duty, there was a discharge for Inability to Adjust to Military Life. No thinking person wanted to be branded with either type of "Other-Than-Honorable" discharge from military service.

However, just as schools must have discipline for any serious learning to take place and armed services must have discipline in order to prepare a cohesive fighting force to protect us from our enemies, a civilization must have discipline to help constrain those who would violate the rules that every civilized society must have to maintain order.

Few would dispute the widely held opinion that the Federal Bureau of Investigation (FBI) has fallen upon hard times. The pristine reputation that Agency held for many years has vanished with the disclosures coming out daily which demonstrate Agents and administrators high up in the Bureau have leaked information, lied and sent text messages to fellow Agents highly critical of Presidential candidate and now President Donald Trump. Regardless whether you are for or against Trump, you should know that Agents of the FBI are charged with the responsibility of being strictly apolitical. For many years, it stayed that way, in spite of the carping you hear on left-leaning television networks and read in liberal-leaning newspapers. To a man—or woman—every member of the Progressive party detested and still do love to hate the original Director of the FBI, J. Edgar Hoover. He might very well have been the anti-Christ, except that most Progressives claim not to believe in God in any aspect.

If you were to look up a description for a mean, vile, crooked, avarice-driven man in a Progressive dictionary, there would be Mr. Hoover's picture as the perfect example. As writer Mark Twain wrote of a newspaper reporting his own death—"Reports of my death are greatly exaggerated."—so could those who knew John Edgar Hoover say about reports of how horrible a man he was—those stories have been greatly exaggerated. Whatever he did that is worthy of criticism, one thing he accomplished as Director of the FBI is that he established an iron discipline in that organization and its Agents. In many respects, the Bureau was quasi-military. For instance, in response to the seemingly minor infraction of misspelling a word in an FBI report that was to be disseminated outside the Bureau, (particularly the office of the President!) the writer of that report might have a projected future raise held up for six months or a year. Costly. For a slightly more serious error, that Agent might find himself and his family uprooted and transferred to a distant office of assignment. He would be given a maximum of 30 days to sell his house, make arrangements to have his furniture picked up, find, hopefully, suitable accommodations in the city to which he had been assigned, and report for duty in that office. Terrible, you say! Draconian, even!

Perhaps so, but if you were to read a report written by an Agent in 1970 and compare it with one written today, you might see anything from a minor to a drastic difference in the style, verbiage, clarity and spelling. The purpose for writing many reports was to outline the evidence that had been collected by the writer and others in preparation for filing charges and eventually prosecuting the subject of the report. That report must be cogent, logically sequential, clear as to what part of the U S Code that person was accused of violating, and easily understood by the United States Attorney or his Assistant who was to be in charge of the prosecution. To have errors in the report was a reflection on the competence of the Agent, a reflection upon the office to which he was assigned, a reflection on the FBI... and Mr. Hoover frowned on anything that reflected unfavorably on his FBI. So you did the job right. Perhaps it was the threat of disciplinary actions that was the prime motivation for doing a good job, but the FBI recruited men and women who embraced the idea that the FBI was a singularly outstanding investigative outfit—the best in the world.

Discipline is imperative in any military unit, football team, classroom, business, industry—or government. What separates the good teams from the also-rans? Often, it is the discipline to expect more from yourselves and the willingness to pay the price to be the best. You have probably heard this saying attributed to several disparate individuals, but it goes like this:

> *If you think you can, or you think you cannot, you are probably right.*

Attitude and confidence in oneself go a long way towards the achievement of a goal. Likewise, the expectations—real, not feigned—of a superior can instill pride of accomplishment and determination to attain a goal difficult of achievement. That means they must work hard even on those days when they do not feel like working at all. Personal discipline often will not allow them to give themselves a day off when there is so much more to be done—not once they see that they are capable. We are to expect the very best from ourselves and have the discipline to pursue that best with all our might. Discipline allows you to develop the habit of honesty, integrity, truth, courage, honor, respect for the rights of others and strength to see that the rights of those weaker among us are not abridged.

What is the antithesis of discipline? Look at the hooligans parading as anti-fascists, who call themselves "Antifa." How do they demonstrate that they are against fascism? By employing the very fascist tactics they profess to oppose in the bullying of their enemies—usually, those attempting to peacefully demonstrate for freedom of speech—by beating the hell out of them with clubs. You will have noticed that these beatings of unarmed demonstrators have sometimes taken place in full view of law enforcement officers, who have been instructed by city, county or state officials to "not interfere." While the cowardly city/county/state and perhaps even federal officials who issue that kind of instructions to the people charged with protecting *all* our citizens is deeply disturbing, the thing that is even more disturbing is that so-called "peace officers" *obey* those unlawful orders.

Children in modern schools will likely not have heard of the Nuremberg Trials conducted of German Nazi criminals at the close of WWII. That important international trial firmly established that the fact German soldiers were *told* to commit atrocities against civilians did not excuse their *carrying out* those orders. The guilty soldiers' consciences should have informed them that the acts they were asked to commit were unlawful and inhuman. They violated a much higher law.

Americans must have the discipline to do what is right, no matter what our political and civic leaders instruct us to do. Are our children being taught that in schools today? This may be a good time to establish something which we seem as a nation to have forgotten: Christians are instructed by the Bible and the teachings of Jesus to obey properly constituted authorities. The reasoning is that those leaders are in the positions they occupy only because of the benevolence of God. If it were not at least in the permissive (as opposed to "direct") will of God, that person would not be in a position of leadership. The only time a Christian is to disobey the civil authorities is when he is instructed to commit an act that would be in direct violation of one of God's laws. The law of God takes precedence over the laws of man.

The following is an excerpt from an article written by Dr. Thomas Sowell, published by Real Clear Politics on March 7, 2006 and entitled *Cathedrals and Faith:*

In crisis, some have to put their lives on the line, as fireman, policemen and people in the military still do. But, for that, you have to believe that the institution and the society are worthy of your sacrifices.

We have now been through at least two generations of constant denigration of American society, two generations in which cheap glory could be gained by flouting rules and mocking values.

Is it surprising that we seem to have dwindling numbers of people willing to take responsibility and make sacrifices to preserve the social framework that makes our survival and advancement possible? Harvard is just one small example.

There was a time when being at war meant accepting a great weight of responsibility, even among politicians. After Wendell Willkie waged a tough presidential election campaign against Franklin D. Roosevelt in 1940, winning more votes than any Republican ever had before, nevertheless after it was all over, he became FDR's personal envoy to Winston Churchill.

In the midst of war today, we see former presidents and defeated presidential candidates telling the world how wrong we are — sometimes collecting big bucks in foreign countries for doing so — and members of Congress playing demagogic party politics with national security.

We still have the cathedral of freedom but how long will it last without the faith?

Copyright 2006 Creators Syndicate

Some of you may remember when demonstrators against the war in Vietnam and other causes large and small were encouraged to engage in "civil disobedience." These demonstrators had no qualms about violating civil law, but felt it was wrong to punish them for such violations. Indeed, they should have been punished—just as Christians who choose to violate a civil law that is in direct conflict with the law of God. All believers must write this upon their hearts in Capital Letters: When there is punishment for violating civil law, the Christian is to accept that punishment. If you ever believed that being a Christian would never bring you into conflict with civil law, you must disabuse yourself of that idea. Unless things are turned around in a manner that is almost impossible to imagine, you are almost certain to find yourself being given instructions by civil authorities that a Christian cannot obey. At that point, you must have the courage and devotion to God to choose to follow His law when it conflicts with civilian authority. Then you are to accept the punishment the civil authorities impose upon you for that supposed violation. Can you do that? *Will* you do that?

Do the majority of Americans desire a government that would instruct Christian people to follow the law, even if that law is in direct violation of God's law? If that is indeed the case, and it someday might well be if it isn't already, the Christian must obey the law of the land not by obeying when it is in direct conflict with the law of God but by submitting to the punishment prescribed for that violation. In other words, he is not to violate the law of God, but he is to be willing to suffer the consequences of his choice when he violates state law. There is no such thing as "civil disobedience" wherein the perpetrator can reasonably expect that the government will not prosecute him for a minor (?) violation. While this is the language of the old-time criminal and not that of a follower of Jesus, the message is applicable to both: "You do the crime, you do the time."

So let me ask you, what sort of government do we want in America? One that is just and seeks to be fair in the application of the law, or one that favors one or the other group while punishing to the full extent of the law those who happen to have another opinion? You see, some forms of government cannot be maintained simply by passing laws making thus-and-so illegal.

Judging by the number of laws we have on the book, it must be assumed that America is one of the most corrupt nations in the world. Our Congress, still not satisfied with the laws on the books, pass many new laws in every congressional term. Several of these are duplications of laws previously passed and simply not enforced. We would have to triple the number of law enforcement officers we have and would still be unable to enforce every law we have on the book.

However, if I may refer back to the two types of discipline of which we spoke earlier, there is a *third* type of discipline or self-control. This, too, is one we impose upon ourselves, but it is applied for an altogether different reason. This is where the importance of Christianity comes in. This self-control is based upon our consideration of the worth of every individual as a child of God and respect for the rights of that person.

For those of you who teach or have taught in our public—even private— schools, are there some students who make it easy for you to love them? Yes. They are well-behaved, polite, considerate, and always have their work in on time.

Then there are the others. Those who seem to just dare you to love them. Maybe their parents or the people with whom they live or stay are not loving toward them and do not take proper care of their physical and emotional needs. You might say there is at least some justification for their bad attitude, sullenness and anger. If you are or were the kind of teacher you should be, you understand that *this* is the child who really needs to be loved. He needs someone to show concern for him, care about his life situation and give him encouragement to face life's challenges. To greet him every day with a smile... I almost said, "And a hug," but you know you can't do that anymore, can you?

When my older brother and I were around the age of ten and eleven, a boy about our age came over to our house on horseback and asked if my brother and I wanted to ride three miles or so to a creek and go swimming. We had horses and, of course, we wanted to go! So we went inside and put the proposition to our mother. She immediately nixed the deal, saying we were too young to go that far and swim unsupervised. We begged and pleaded, but as usual her decision was final. We came out of the house all downcast, kicking at the ground and complaining. I looked up at the other boy's face and saw a big tear sliding down his cheek. He said, "I wish my mother cared where I go and what I do."

Ouch!

Sometimes love requires us to care enough to say , "No" when we would give anything to be able to say, "Yes."

Chapter 26

THE AMERICAN BOOMERANG

Brave, free, and independent men and women created a system of voluntary cooperation where all progressed, catalyzing the most prosperous country on Earth. That's America!
—*PANAM Post, 11/13/19*

BELOW IS AN excerpt from a Townhall.com article by Kara Jones entitled "American Exceptionalism—the World's Greatest 'Turnaround' Nation Will Do It Again."

English author G. K. Chesterton once wrote, "America is the only nation in the world that is founded on a creed... It enunciates that all men are equal in their claim to justice, that governments exist to give them that justice, and that their authority is for that reason just."

The creed Chesterton refers to is, of course, the Declaration of Independence. This endowing document approved by Congress 238 years ago tomorrow, July 4, proclaims that all people are created free and equal.

Sadly, an entire generation of young Americans is emerging from our schools and universities that is no longer being taught what it means to be an American. The cries of political correctness and the one world movement insist that teachers and professors not acknowledge excellence, either for individuals or for our country. It is all an effort to level the playing field.

However, much is to be said for American exceptionalism. The truth is that in 5,000 years of recorded human history, there has never before been a nation like America. A leader throughout the agricultural, industrial, and technological eras, America stands alone in the advancement of human innovation. When we think of America's inventive genius, our country is responsible for the birth of technologies used around the world every day: personal computers, the Internet, GPS, the light bulb, the telephone, and the airplane.

This is the case made by Nick Adams, the youngest Deputy Mayor in Australian history in Sydney, at the age of twenty-one. Nick is a best-selling author, columnist and commentator, all achieved before he turned 30. He believes it is "high time" for an outsider to speak to Americans' hearts and outline to them what makes their country great.

Adams has written a book entitled *The American Boomerang*, in which he defends his adopted country.

Yesterday [July 2, 2014] at the Heritage Foundation, Adams said:

> *"I'm here to give Americans optimism at a time where there are so many slumped shoulders. I must say that if I were an American, I would also feel that there is not much reason to be hopeful. I think it is indisputable that America is in decline as we speak. But decline, I believe, is a choice, it's not a condition. Decline can be reversed. A lot of America's current ailments are a result, I think, of policy failures. To use an Australian term, I think that America can boomerang provided that it re-embraces the values and the virtues of its founding principles and its history.*
>
> *"Many of you might wonder why an Australian with a funny accent would want to write a book about American greatness and why an Australian would even care what happens to America. The answer to that is very simple: What is good for America is good for the world. When America is strong, the world is strong. When America is weak, the world is weak. When America is weak, the world is dangerous. The less powerful America is, the more harmful the world will be. And that's why I believe it's in the interest of everyone, no matter where they live, to stand up and fight for America."*

Americans must rally and preserve our distinct value system if we are to *"boomerang back to greatness."* Adams observes:

> *It's optimism, not pessimism. It's patriotism, not relativism. It's faith, not secularism. It's life, not death. It's*

E Pluribus Unum, not multiculturalism. It's individualism, not collectivism. It's equality of opportunity, not equality of outcome.

They are the things that have made America so different, they are the things that have catapulted America to incredible heights, and they are the values that will see America boomerang back to greatness.

What will it take for America to boomerang? Adams explains that Americans need to unite behind a consensus-inspiring agenda.

That agenda must be ending the waste, paying back the debt, axing political correctness, limiting the government, protecting the borders, preserving Judeo-Christian values, ending the culture of entitlement, cutting taxes, keeping the peace by unquestioned military advantage, and exercising fidelity to the Constitution.

Chapter 27

THE ERA OF THE CHURCH

*Not forsaking the gathering of ourselves together as
the manner of some is, but exhorting one another,
and so much the more as ye see the day approaching...*
—Hebrews 10:25, Scofield Reference Bible

NOT LONG AGO, in the historical perspective, at least in the
south and middle western states, no school or civic activity was
scheduled that would be in conflict with local church services. That
is probably hard for those of you under fifty years of age to believe,
but it is true. Many states, counties and cities had so-called "Blue
Laws" that forbade the selling of alcoholic beverages on Sundays.
Most stores were closed on Sundays, including grocery and drug
stores. You could have rolled up the city sidewalks for storage on
Sundays in many of our American cities for lack of traffic.

The thought behind the measures listed above was that city officials did not want to inhibit a citizen's opportunity to attend church
services on that day. Church attendance was valued that highly in
the late Forties and early Fifties. Perhaps the most respected person
in small towns and cities was the pastor of the local church or the
priest of the local Catholic Church.

Perhaps it is coincidental that among the forty-five goals of
Communism in America are numbers 27 and 28, and that these goals
are in perfect harmony with the ideas of the secular humanists, even

if they do not have discernible ties with Communism or Socialism. They believe that man needs no god, no moral or religious authority. It is convenient for those two groups (Communists/Socialists and Secular Humanists) that their animosity toward Christianity is a shared sentiment.

27. Infiltrate the churches and replace revealed religion with "social" religion. Discredit the Bible and emphasize the need for intellectual maturity, which does not need a "religious crutch." – DONE AND CONTINUING

28. Eliminate prayer or any phase of religious expression in the schools on the ground that it violates the principle of "separation of church and state." – DONE

Let's face it—the primary hurdle that an intellectual or someone steeped in the belief that acceptance of an idea or philosophy depends upon its ability to be demonstrated through science is the acceptance of a world with which they have no familiarity. That is the realm of the spiritual. To them, if you cannot see it or demonstrate it through science it is not true.

It is tedious and counterproductive to point out the myriad things we accept every day without being able to prove them through science, such as the doctor you trust to perform a complicated and dangerous brain surgery upon you without the benefit of knowing pre-surgery that he will be successful and you will live through the process. You may say, "Undergoing that surgery is my only option if I am to live." A Christian might counter, "Giving your heart and soul to Jesus Christ is the only way you can live eternally."

You do not believe in a life after death?

If that is the case—if you are absolutely certain that there is no life after death, can you prove that to me scientifically? Where are your facts to come from? Is there someone you know who has died and now can provide you incontrovertible, unimpeachable proof that he was a Christian when he died and did not awake after death in the presence of Jesus? No?

How can you prove the un-provable? Science is of no value in that situation. What Christians know is that the existence of Christ can only be "proven" by faith.

"Faith." That is a word that has almost been excluded from the lexicon of most Americans.

But it was faith that persuaded you to undergo the dangerous brain surgery we mentioned. Faith that the doctor's skill would suffice, and that the result would be a whole "you" without the dangerous affliction from which you had suffered.

A Christian's faith is in the efficacy of Christ to deliver the salvation He promised; the salvation of the most important part of any of us—our soul. Our body wears out; sooner than many of us are prepared to accept. But our soul shall live forever in the presence of God.

Bah. It is foolish to believe that hogwash!

Perhaps. However, if we (Christians) are right and you as an unbeliever are wrong, the consequences of your error are devastating—and eternal.

Yes, but look at all the life you will have missed out on if I am right and your faith is in error.

Ah, that is the beautiful part about being a follower of Jesus. You do not miss out on a single thing that is beautiful, enjoyable and productive. I, like you, know some Christian men who look as though they had just eaten a whole lemon, or perhaps an unripe persimmon, their face is so long and sad-looking, I also know many Christians whose joy is so complete and transparent that it is written all over their faces. Men and women whose lives have been redeemed by the Lord of all creation. They fully comprehend that they are not of this world. Their home is in heaven with the Lord Jesus Christ. They are only brief travelers on this sphere.

Shakespeare had Macbeth say, "Life's but a walking shadow, a poor player that struts and frets his hour upon the stage and then is heard no more: it is a tale told by an idiot, full of sound and fury, signifying nothing."

When the end of our life comes, if we die without having accepted Jesus Christ as our Lord and Master, that declaration of Macbeth is true for each of us.

The Bible says in Matthew 16:26 – "For what is a man profited, if he shall gain the whole world, but loses his soul? Or what will a man give in exchange for his soul?"

Without Jesus, that is the condition of your life—seventy to eighty years of experiencing perhaps the best that the world has to offer, to be followed by an eternity separated from God. In Hell.

Yes, I do believe in a literal Hell. I have few ideas what that place is going to be like, but I have no desire to find out by spending eternity there.

Jesus said it this way: "My kingdom is not of this world: if my kingdom were of this world, then would my servants fight, that I should not be delivered to the Jews: but now is my kingdom not from hence." (John 18:36).

We as Christians are to live in this world, but we are not of this world.

We—human beings, *Homo sapiens*—are spiritual beings, in addition to our physical characteristics. It is to this, our spiritual aspect, that Jesus came to "seek and to save." It is far more important than our physical presence. We will live, most of us, only seventy or eighty years on this earth. Think about this for a moment: if there is a life after death, we are told that there is no end to that afterlife. Eternity—a difficult concept to grasp. Yet if it is for real, who would opt to spend eternity in Hell when he has the opportunity to spend forever in the presence of God? I am aware that some Christians' description of what they consider heaven will be like is not all that appealing, sitting around in a circle singing songs of praise to God. We certainly will be doing that, but do you really suppose that a God who loved you so much that He sent His only Son to die for your sins—do you think that God would have you spend eternity bored to tears and unhappy? If you think that, you don't serve the God that I know. Heaven will be a place of supreme joy, happiness and freedom from pain, want or sorrow.

You might not be at all interested in knowing how a lost person— one who has not come to a saving relationship with Jesus Christ— can become a Christian, but I am going to take a stab at explaining the plan of salvation to you none the less.

Reverend Billy Graham, at least one of the best-known evangelists in America history, had a very simple explanation for why one needed Jesus, and how to become a Christian. Graham would cite Bible passages that explain how all have sinned and fallen short of the glory of God. Then he would explain that the wages of sin— what those sins have earned for you—is death—separation from God. He would proceed to explain how God loved you so much that He sent His only-begotten Son to "seek and to save the lost"; to literally die in your stead so that you would not have to face the penalty of sin—death—, but that Christ's atoning death paid the penalty of your sins and made you wholly acceptable in God's sight.

The following is what Christians call "The Roman Road," because it is a list of verses from the Biblical book of Romans, written by the Apostle Paul, outlining how a lost person might become a Christian.

> Romans 3:10 – "As it is written, there is none righteous; no, not one." And...

> Romans 3:23 – "For all have sinned and come short of the glory of God."

Anyone who has lived on this earth, with the singular exception of Jesus Christ, has sinned against God—that is, has committed acts contrary to God's will. There is no way to be completely sinless in a sinful world. Those first two verses, then, apply to each of us. There is not one thing that any of us can do to earn or deserve eternal life.

Only a perfect person, a saint, can live in the presence of God. We know that living a perfect life is not possible (I'll have a little caveat on that subject later).

So how can *anyone* be saved?

Romans 5:8 – "But God commendeth (extends; gives) His love toward us in that while we were yet sinners, Christ died for us."

Perhaps here we need to interject some facts about who and what God is. God is omnipotent (suzerainty, rule, ownership over everything), omniscient (sees all and knows all), omnipresent (everywhere at the same time; all-encompassing) and pure (sinless, perfect; unable to even look upon sin). In order to enjoy life in the presence of God, you must be sinless.

Impossible! That means nobody can be saved!

Obviously, God knows our hearts. Israel's King David wrote in Psalms 139:13 – "For you formed my inward parts; you knitted me together in my mother's womb." How well does God know you? Perfectly.

Romans 5:12 – "Wherefore, as by one man (Adam) sin entered into the world, and death by sin; and so death passed upon all men, for that all have sinned." Then...

Romans 6:23 – "For the wages of sin is death; but the gift of God is eternal life through Jesus Christ our Lord."

What we have earned is that we deserve death because of our sin. But the God whose very perfection makes it impossible for us to earn or deserve our salvation not only demands perfection but supplies the propitiation (atonement, salvation, buying out of Hell, as it were) through Jesus Christ, His Son.

Romans 10:9-11 – "That if thou shalt confess with thy mouth the Lord Jesus, and shalt believe in thine heart that God hath raised Him from the dead, thou shalt be saved. For with the heart man believeth unto righteousness; and with the mouth confession is made unto salvation. For the scripture saith, whosoever believeth on Him shall not be ashamed." More emphatically...

Romans 10:13 – "For whoever shall call upon the name of the Lord shall be saved."

So... How does one become a Christian?

1) Admit you are a sinner and confess (admit) that to God in prayer. I John 1:8 – "If we say we have no sin, we deceive ourselves, and the truth is not in us."

2) Repent of those sins. You must be genuinely sorry for the sins you have committed against God—and you must tell Him so.

3) Understand that salvation is available only through Jesus Christ. John 14:6 – "Jesus said unto him, 'I am the way, the truth and the life; no man comes unto the Father, but by me." I Timothy 2:5 – "For there is one God, and one mediator between God and men, the man Jesus." Acts 4:7 – "Neither is there salvation in any other; for there is none other name under heaven given among men whereby we must be saved."

4) Pray that Jesus Christ might come into your heart—accept the free gift of eternal life through Him.

Reverend Billy Graham would tell any lost person, "Believe in the Lord Jesus Christ, and you shall be saved." He would likely quote some or all of the verses above explaining the simple plan of salvation, then ask you to confess your sins, repent of those sins and call upon the name of Jesus, asking Him to forgive those sins;

to come into your heart and save you. He would lead you in what he called "a believer's prayer." That prayer might go something like this: "Lord Jesus, I know that I am a sinner, and those sins I confess to you that I have committed and ask you, Father, to forgive me those sins and to save me. Lord Jesus, would you right now come into my heart?"

It's as simple as that.

There is one other verse from the Bible that I must not omit.

If you were to ask one hundred Christians what is their favorite verse, it is likely that sixty of those would claim this verse as their most beloved:

> John 3:16 – "For God so loved the world that He gave his only begotten Son, that whosoever believeth in Him should not perish, but have everlasting life."

To personalize this verse, as God would have you hear it, substitute your name for the words, "the world," so that it would read, for me, "For God so loved Bill Brown that He gave His only begotten Son..." Because the truth is, should you be the only individual on earth standing in need of God's grace and His redemptive gift, God would have sent His Son for you alone. That is how much He loves you. YOU!

Do you really believe that you would have to give up much in life that is enjoyable to serve a God who loved you so much? It is because of that great love He has for you that He wants the very best for you, not the worst. Think of it this way—would you as a father or mother seek ways in which you might make your child's life miserable?

Whoops! I've been a polygraph examiner too long to ask such a question; of course, I have dealt with people who have done just that. This is not, however, the norm. Most parents are much more likely to be overindulgent rather than cruel and depriving with their children.

If we, then, *who scarcely know how to love,* would try to see that our children are happy, healthy and well-fed, how much more would the Heavenly Father who sent His only Son to die for us—"while we were yet sinners"—seek only what is the very best for His children for whom He paid the ultimate price?

There is a beautiful old hymn, based, as many of them are, on Bible scripture—"The Ninety and Nine". It goes something like this:

> There were ninety and nine who safely lay
> In the shelter of the fold.
> But one was out on the hills away,
> Far off from the gates of gold
> Away on the mountains, wild and bare,
> Away from the Shepherd's tender care.

The song ends with the Angels singing, "Rejoice, for the Shepherd brings back His own." He sought for and found His one lost sheep and returned it safely to the fold.

You see, no matter how many millions or billions accept Christ as their Savior, God is not willing that any should be lost, or perish. He is constantly seeking—for you, if you do not know Christ as your Savior.

In the best way I know how, I have explained how to become a Christian. The incentives to do so are obvious—beyond what some refer to as "fire insurance"—avoiding an eternity in Hell. Living a life as close to the center of God's will is the most perfect, the most peaceful, the most enjoyable life there is.

Why don't more of us live there, instead of skulking in the shadows, ashamed to be called a Christian? That is an excellent question, even considering I am the one who asked it. I wish I had a good answer.

The answer is very simple, and at the same time complicated as it can be. If you believe the Bible is God's word, you have the assurance of the indwelling Holy Spirit. Indwelling—that is, in your very soul, communicating with you as often and as freely as you allow Him to. He—the Holy Spirit—is capable of empowering you to complete any task that God has set for you. God will not assign a job to you that He cannot enable you to succeed in accomplishing. The Holy Spirit also communicates to God when we know not how to pray or what to say to God. The Holy Spirit is an intercessor.

Romans 8:26-27 says, "Likewise, the Spirit also helpeth our infirmity, for we know not what we should pray for as we ought; but the Spirit himself maketh intercession for us with groaning which cannot be uttered. 27 And he that searcheth the hearts knoweth what is the mind of the Spirit, because he maketh intercession for the saints (believers) according to the will of God."

Admittedly, I have written a great deal more about Christianity than any of the other religions of the world. One reason for that is that I know more about Christianity than about any other belief. The second and more compelling reason is that I firmly believe that Christianity provides the most solid, dependable, promising basis upon which individuals, families, communities and nations can place their trust and build their futures.

Now, wait a minute, you might say. Are you telling me an individual can *really* place his trust in the hope of salvation through faith in Jesus Christ? Can you really put that kind of blind trust in an individual you have never seen and whose very existence is disputed by many learned people?

Well, yes, as a matter of fact. Yes, you can!

It was just before 8:00 AM Monday morning, April 24, 1978. I had just returned the day before from Quantico, Virginia, where I had attended a training session on how to perform the duties of Principle Firearms Instructor and was to assume those duties for the Oklahoma City Division of the FBI. A month earlier, I had hardly known what a PFI was. Now I am one.

That morning, we began the process of helping more than 50 officers qualify with a revolver of .38 caliber or better by the next Friday afternoon—4 days hence. Nobody had gotten permission from the Oklahoma City Police Department to use their firearms range, so as a poor third choice, we ended up doing firearms training in the basement of the Law Enforcement Training Center in Oklahoma City.

That afternoon, each officer was issued six dummy rounds. (bullets from which the primer has been removed and that hole filled with Elmer's glue, making the round inert. It has the same weight and feel of a regular round, except that it does not fire when the firing pin hits the place where the primer had been). I had the officers line up around the walls of the gym. Their instructions were to hold an empty weapon (unloaded with ammunition) at the ready, and at the whistle, simulate firing six rounds from the "hip" position at an imaginary target. Then they were to open the cylinder of the weapon (only revolvers, in that day), simulate dumping those 6 empty casings, reload with 6 of these inert wadcutter rounds, close the cylinder, resume the hip-shooting position and pull the trigger 6 more times at that imaginary target.

Do you have the picture?

When my stopwatch sweep hand reached the top, I blew the whistle to begin the exercise. You could hear triggers snapping all over the gym. In 10 to 15 seconds, the first of them opened the cylinder, turned the weapon upside down and shook it as though to empty the cylinder, and began loading with the inert rounds. I heard the first of these click the cylinder back into place, and only a moment later—"POW!"

The person who stood just 10 feet to my left happened to be one of the first to reload with the dummy rounds, and the first one he pulled the trigger on was... not inert, but a live round!

I heard the shot and felt a blow to the left side of my head. As I was going down, I ran my tongue around the inside of my mouth, hoping to find a few busted or missing teeth. I could live (literally!) with that. No such luck.

Blood was gushing from my mouth and nose like a wide-open fire hydrant.

I quickly realized I would not live long enough for the ambulance EMTs to come inside and find me, so I made for the gym exit, skating in a trail of blood almost three feet wide in front of me. I couldn't breathe. My trachea reflexively closed itself off against the backward pressure of the blood. My heart was hammering in my chest. It occurred to me that I must get my blood pressure under control or I'd bleed to death in minutes.

Scared? Yes, I was scared. Most of us fear death, even if it is only dread of the greatest unknown. I'm no hero.

What do you do to calm yourself when you are certain you are going to die?

Did you ever hear of anyone getting shot with a .38 round above the mouth and surviving? Neither had I.

I pushed through a set of swinging doors into the hallway and sat down in the floor, leaned forward a little, and began to do some soul-searching.

First, I am a Christian. I knew without a doubt where I was going the moment I died.

Secondly, my wife is a Christian; of that I was certain.

Third, I had the privilege of leading all three of our children in praying to ask Jesus Christ into their hearts to save them. They were all secure in Christ.

Fourth, within two days of my death, an FBI Agent would deliver a check to my wife to handle expenses until she would begin receiving a large percentage of my paycheck for as long as she lived. My family's future was financially secure.

By the time an EMT from upstairs got down to where I was sitting, the bleeding had slowed dramatically, and when he took my blood pressure, it was 121-70; pulse 60.

The fear was gone, I was prepared to die; even began to feel good about it, to look forward to it! Crazy? No. Confident and at peace.

Again, I am not a particularly brave man. But faith in the Christ who freely gave me salvation was strong enough that it was not difficult for me to say, "Lord Jesus, I happily come to you." I am neither strong nor brave—but He is!

Chapter 28

HOW CAN CHRISTIANS HELP AMERICA?

THERE IS A far greater alternative to the "one-world" philosophy, the "moral equivalency," and the vacuous emptiness of secular humanism. It is a life of hope, placed in the Lord Jesus Christ who has secured not only our eternal salvation but has authored a far greater manner of living than that bound up in ourselves. He offers the daily, moment-to-moment help of the Holy Spirit to reinforce our desire and our ability to treat others as we would have others treat us; to love others as Jesus loves them and to make a positive contribution to the people around us.

Let us illustrate firm conviction of God's power and grace by living lives reflective of God's love. What that would require of us is that we love one another, even as Jesus loves us.

> John 13:35 – "By this shall all men know that ye are
> my disciples, if ye have love one to another."

Have you ever wondered how you might serve God? What need does He have that your service to Him might meet?

That's right—none.

So how do we serve Him? One way is for us to serve others. People have needs. We have needs. To serve others is one way for us to render service to God.

Jesus said in Matt: 25:40 – "...Verily I say unto you, inasmuch as ye have done it unto one of the least of these my brethren, ye have done it unto me."

As Christians, we are to strive to reflect God's goodness and mercy in our own lives. Treat others not as equals but as betters. If that sounds a little odd to you, perhaps you will have never heard an old acronym from many years ago. It was "J-O-Y," and it stood for Jesus, Others and You. That is the way to achieve pure joy in your life. Just as God's kingdom is not of this world, His way of serving rather than being served is an example of how dramatic is the difference between what is deemed desirable in this world and what is to be sought in God's realm. Just as it truly is better to give than to receive, it is better by far to serve than to be served.

Can you imagine how much influence thousands, hundreds of thousands, millions of Christians emulating Christ to the best of their ability would have on the average citizen in our country? I have a feeling those who choose this path will find many pejorative appellations hung around their necks when they begin to act in the way all believers should have been acting since first accepting Jesus. But they should pay no thought to what others say. Rather, they are to pray constantly and seek the guidance of the indwelling Holy Spirit, because there is no way to live a life that is pleasing to God without the strength, grace and courage that the Holy Spirit of God provides. While we can perform no service to God in our own strength, the Apostle Paul tells us in the Book of Philippians 4:13 – "I can do all things in Him (Christ) who strengthens me."

We must dare to be different.

Certainly one of the factors that deters us in serving God daily is the fear of ridicule from the secularists and humanists who dominate our schools and universities and occupy almost every important position of authority in our major media outlets, print and visual. Since they are their own gods, they certainly can see no reason someone should waste his time worshiping a fictitious entity who is simply a figment of someone's active imagination.

Why then should a believer pay any heed at all to someone who has no earthly idea what he is talking about when it comes to spiritual matters?

Receiving criticism from a secular humanist relative to your Christian walk is somewhat akin to reading a critique on the New York Philharmonic Orchestra written by a man with a tin ear. Of what possible value would that be?

The Christian struggle is with himself; to do as the Apostle Paul demanded and "die to self" is just as real as it is difficult.

> "I am crucified with Christ: nevertheless I live; yet not I, but Christ liveth in me: and the life which I now live in the flesh I live by the faith of the Son of God, who loved me, and gave himself for me."
> Galatians 2:20.

In another place, Paul said, "For me to live is Christ, and to die is gain."–Philippians 1:21. He believed it would be better from a selfish standpoint for him to die and go to be with Christ Jesus. However, if it were better for the ones whom Paul shepherded in the faith for him to continue that work, he was willing and eager.

Oh, but that is so difficult—even to hear, let alone hope to accomplish. That is what Jesus asks of us, however. We are to place all emphasis on the spiritual facet of our being and "lay up for ourselves treasures in heaven." Remember the brevity of this life on earth compared to eternity in heaven, which is our home. We are sojourners here on earth, trying to learn what God would have us do with our lives.

One of the things I am persuaded He would ask of us, though I lay no claim on any ability to look into the mind of our Lord, is to learn that difficult lesson of how to die to self and live unto the Lord. It means, among other things, that we are to be far less concerned with how we are treated, what happens to us day by day (don't be dismayed when you are "dissed") and be far more concerned with making the lives of others a bit more bearable. We can live a victorious, joyful life wherein Christ is reflected in our looks and in our actions; in everything we do. He (Jesus) must increase, but I must decrease. Daily.

You have heard it said that we are to "cast your bread (something good or kind or a service for another person) upon the water, and it shall not return to you void." Each selfless service you perform to lighten someone's burden or to brighten his day or to help feed his family, without expecting anything in return, might cause others to wonder from whence the strength and love to impel you to do that kindness. At that point, they may be led to understand that only the love of Christ can allow you to perform an act of complete selflessness. This is not an attribute that I have without the influence of God's Holy Spirit enabling me. I am not naturally good, or normally kind or generous. To the extent that I should ever demonstrate any of those qualities, you may be sure that I am acting under the influence of the Holy Spirit of God.

We mentioned earlier that the Holy Spirit comes to take up residency in your soul the moment you ask Jesus Christ into your heart and obtain His salvation; totally by grace (unearned; it is a free gift of God). The Holy Spirit is not a pushy boarder. He will not command you or nag you, in the strictest sense of that word. He will, however, never let you alone. He will be constantly available to help you accomplish a job, a purpose or an act for which you may be in no way prepared. He will scare you to death, but when you follow his direction and attempt what you know in your heart God is asking of you, you will find that while you might not possess the skill to perform that act, God will supply your every need. He will never ask you to do anything in his behalf without giving you all the skills, talents—even the words you are supposed to say to accomplish His will. He will never fail you.

If you have no concept of a spiritual being, you can ill understand the principles of Jesus, who emphatically informed Roman and Jewish authorities alike that His kingdom was not of this world but was rather a realm of the spirit. A self-possessed secular humanist would be unaware of any need he might have of a spiritual guide and could not possibly be persuaded that the *spiritual* facet of his life was far more important than the physical or worldly. In the belief of a Christian, his tenure on earth is but a preparation for eternity in the presence of God. Think about that for a moment... How long is eternity?

The point is, Christians should not be unduly troubled by the ridicule and disdain shown them by secularists. They have no concept of your world. Do you recall the semi-hysteria among members of the press corps when former President Jimmy Carter informed them that he had been "born again"? They didn't know whether to laugh or send for the men with the net and the long-sleeved jacket that buckles in the back. Most of them had not a clue as to what he was referring.

Since we are born of the Spirit and will spend eternity (Do you have your mind wrapped around that concept yet?) in heaven, it makes perfect sense that we Christians should be about developing the spiritual facet of our lives in preparation for eternity in heaven.

That brings up another important if peripheral subject. How can secularists or non-Christians of any stripe critique how successful the Christian has been in following God's will and plan for his life? Without a personal relationship with the Creator and sans critical information from the Christian bible, how can they have any idea what God expects of His people? Indeed, how are we as believers equipped to discern upon what criteria God judges the acts of His children? Answer—we are not.

Can an individual, Christian or no, struggling along with a very finite mind have any concept what an infinite God is thinking? We cannot, but remember that God knows everything about each of us. Everything. Do not deceive yourself that you have any secrets from God. I do not understand how God can be everywhere at once, hear each of the perhaps billion prayers uttered at any one moment, have a count on every hair (disappearing rapidly from my head), and have an awareness of everything going on in all the universe. I simply know that He does all these things and infinitely more. There was a beautiful old song I once heard Ethel Waters sing called, "His Eye is On the Sparrow," which ended with the assurance,

> His eye is on the sparrow,
> And I know He watches me.

We cannot understand all the aspects—should I say any facet—of God's judgment regarding our daily acts. When you bring to mind the terrible sins you think you have committed against God and in His sight, you are encouraged to recall that through the prophet Samuel, God said about King David, "He is a man after mine own heart." David, who not only committed adultery with Bathsheba but also sent her soldier husband Uriah to the place at the front where the fighting was fiercest so that he would almost certainly be killed in battle. That act was tantamount to murder. Yet God placed His imprimatur on David. Was He giving His stamp of approval on either of these or any other sinful acts of David? No, we must know that God saw something in David's heart and soul that pleased Him. It is a reminder that all our sins, egregious as they might be, are washed away in the sacrificial blood of Jesus Christ.

Maybe God looks at a man's inward-most heart and soul; not at the outward appearance, things that mere man might see. God is not fooled by our actions or words. In the Book of Samuel, God had looked at King Saul's heart and rejected him. God had looked at David's heart and chosen him.

> Now the LORD said to Samuel, "How long will you grieve over Saul, since I have rejected him from being king over Israel? Fill your horn with oil and go; I will send you to Jesse the Bethlehemite, for I have selected a king for myself among his sons." (NASB) 1 Samuel 16:1.

By the way, the instruction to "fill your horn with oil" was a reference to the fact the prophet Samuel would be anointing the head of the new King, David, at God's instruction. The horn of a sheep was a vessel often used to carry oil or other liquids.

When Samuel arrived, he was impressed with several of the sons of Jesse. But God did not want them. Finally, God directed him to select the youngest son, David.

> 1 Samuel 16: 10 Thus Jesse made seven of his sons pass before Samuel. But Samuel said to Jesse, "The LORD has not chosen these." 11 And Samuel said to Jesse, "Are these all the children?" And he said, "There remains yet the youngest, and behold, he is tending the sheep." Then Samuel said to Jesse, "Send and bring him; for we will not sit down until he comes here." 12 So he sent and brought him in. Now he was ruddy, with beautiful eyes and a

handsome appearance. And the LORD said, "Arise, anoint him; for this is he." 13 Then Samuel took the horn of oil and anointed him in the midst of his brothers; and the Spirit of the LORD came mightily upon David from that day forward. And Samuel arose and went to Ramah. (NASB) 1 Samuel 16:10-13.

What did God see in the boy David that caused Him to select that child to be king? Nobody but God knows. The important thing is, nobody but God need know what His criteria is when He searches the hearts of man. We would never be able to understand in any event, unless God chose to reveal it to us.

By the way, while we cannot know what criteria God uses to evaluate our actions and thoughts, we do have a significant source of information as to what God would have us do and the behaviors He would elicit from us. That is a function of the Holy Spirit who entered your spirit the moment you accepted Jesus Christ. Jesus told His disciples before His ascension that one of the Holy Spirit's duties is to guide us into all truths about Jesus. Another is that when we know not how to pray as we ought, the Holy Spirit will (Romans 8: 26-27)... "help(s) us in our weakness; for we do not know how to pray as we ought, but the Spirit himself intercedes for us with sighs too deep for words. 27) And He who searches the hearts of men knows what is in the mind of the Spirit, because the Spirit intercedes for the saints (Christians) according to the will of God."

Notice that the Holy Spirit is—believe it or not—a Spirit! Again, Jesus said in John 4:24 "*God* is spirit, and those who worship him must worship in Spirit and in truth."

We Christians should not be overly concerned with the cares of this world, with its attractions and its temptations. Nor should we weep when our plans for the future seem impossible of attainment.

We must keep our eyes upon Jesus and strive to become more like Him day by day. Instead of spending time watching television or playing video games, we should spend more time in prayer and Bible reading. Instead of thinking about the next toy or desirable object we want for ourselves, we should be thinking about how we can be of service to God and to others.

There is nothing more personal than the relationship between a Christian and his Lord. If your critic has never experienced that connection, he can have no idea as to whether your actions as he has observed them are pleasing in God's sight. Further, since that relationship is the most important one you have or will ever have, you should have no regard for what criticism any mere man may throw at you.

There is a wonderful old Christian song entitled, "Victory in Jesus." It presents some very worshipful thoughts and ideas. I'm afraid, however, that not only unbelievers but many Christians are not fully aware or appreciative of one way in which the believer has been handed one of his greatest victories through the atoning death of Jesus—that over self.

This is not easy to accomplish, this death of "self." One of Christianity's most revered apostles, Paul, wrote in Romans 7:15-20: "I do not understand my own actions. For I do not do what I want, but I do the very thing I hate. 16 Now if I do what I do not want, I agree that the law is good. 17 So then it is no longer I that do it, but sin which dwells in me. 18 For I know that nothing good dwells within me, that is, in my flesh. I can will what is right, but I cannot do it. 19 For I do not the good I want, but the evil I do not want is what I do. 20 Now if I do what I do not want, it is no longer I that do it, but sin which dwells within me."

If we skip on down to verse 24, we read, "Wretched man that I am! Who will deliver me from this body of death? Then in verse 25, he answers his own question. 25 Thanks be to God through Jesus

Christ our Lord! So then, I of myself serve the law of God with my mind, but with my flesh I serve the law of sin.

Romans 8: 1-2, "There is therefore now no condemnation for those who are in Christ Jesus. 2 For the law of the Spirit of life in Christ Jesus has set me free from the law of sin and death."

Whoa! That is heavy, even for a committed Christian steeped in the Bible. What Paul is saying is that even after Christ has entered our life and granted us His salvation, we are still under the influence of the OSN.

The what?

OSN. Old Sin Nature.

You see, being possessed with a free will not only means we have a choice regarding whether we accept the grace of God offered in salvation, it also extends to having the free will to decide whether to follow God and allow His Holy Spirit to enable us to serve Jesus Christ.

If you have accepted Christ and He has entered your heart and soul, He has made a difference in your life; you will never be the same person you were prior to salvation. However, He doesn't order your every thought or force you to behave in a manner reflective of what He has done for you. But He has sent the Holy Spirit to indwell your soul and be available to lead you as God would have you act, speak and think.

Left to our own devices, we have a strong tendency to seek only our own comfort and happiness. That is the OSN in action. At least allow me to say this for myself—I am extremely self-centered and self-concerned. It takes an effort of will for me to really care what is going on with you. It hurts me to admit that, but it is nonetheless true. If I am going to be considerate of others and care about their well-being, the impetus for those feelings is not going to come from me, but rather from the Holy Spirit who indwells me. I can't say it any plainer than that.

That is what the Apostle Paul was referring to when he said in I Corinthians 15:31... "I die every day."

Can you really do that? Can you "die to self" and truly live for Christ?

That is the goal. When we take our eyes off ourselves and turn them upon Jesus, then will our lives be full, joyful, and fruitful. Only Jesus Christ empowers us to accomplish that goal.

Secular humanists must be asking, "Why do you want to live for somebody else? You have a life—why not live it to the fullest for yourself!"

The "fullest" life you can ever live is that one wherein you look for opportunities everywhere you turn to ease the heartache and burdens of *another person.*

"That's a bald-faced lie!" you say.

True, we sometimes behave as though it is a dog-eat-dog environment—every man for himself, and the devil take the hind-most!

That is only because we have forgotten the pure pleasure, the absolute joy that comes from doing something for somebody else—particularly when the person you minister to is one who can never return the favor. This is the best form of "witnessing" (remember, we talked about that earlier) in which you may be involved. Secularists are right in this one matter—people are not innately outgoing and interested in the welfare of others, particularly if that "other" is of a different social class or level of educational attainment. Let me emphasize—neither are Christians, in and of themselves. They must be led and filled with the love of God, which is for every human being, regardless of circumstances.

That is the advantage Christians have over any—I repeat, *any*—non-believer; the power of the indwelling Holy Spirit.

Remember what Thomas Jefferson said when he declared that Christians are the best friend of government because "it is the only religion that changes the heart?" Hearts are changed by the intervention of the Holy Spirit—not of one's own volition, but when He is asked to come into your heart and help you to behave, act or speak in a manner more like Jesus. God, through the Holy Spirit, gives you every talent or ability you will need to accomplish His purposes.

When we mature as Christians to the point we may be able to admit that there is no good in us except that which is imputed by Jesus Christ, and we are incapable of accomplishing anything of lasting value without the empowering of the Holy Spirit, then—and only then—we may be useful tools in the hands of our Lord whose desire is to bless us. The Apostle Paul, again, in 2 Corinthians 12:10 said "for when I am weak, then am I strong." When I fully understand that all good things come from the Father and that He must increase daily in importance in my life while I must decrease in the same proportion—then I may be growing. Until I can get my mind focused on the things above and place worldly things in their proper perspective I will be hampered by self.

Until we Christians can earnestly pray with King David the 51st Psalm, vv. 10-12, "Create in me a clean heart, O God, and put a right spirit within me. 11 Cast me not away from Thy presence and take not thy Holy Spirit from me. 12 Restore to me the joy of thy salvation..." we will never fulfill the promise of the Constitutional Republic formed by our Founding Fathers. *As many of those good and brilliant men attested, a Democratic Republic is meant only for a Christian nation and is wholly inapplicable for any other.*

Why? Because a nation so founded and so delicately balanced between three separate but equal branches of government must be led by men and women with courage, discipline, honesty, integrity and a willingness to make personal sacrifices for the benefit of the nation and its people. Those leaders must be motivated to work for the people by a deep and abiding love for the people and for the nation.

I believe it is the duty of Christians and Christian churches to be not just CINOs (Christians In Name Only) but people who live by the word of God. We have been instructed to "Let your light so shine before men, that they may see your good works and give glory to your Father who is in heaven (Matthew 5:16).

If I seem to be pointing a finger at you, let me assure you when my pointed finger is aimed at you, at least three fingers are pointed back at me, because I am one of the most slothful when it comes to spending time with God. Instead of being aware that my advanced age means I have less time to serve God and sort of make amends for my former lassitude, I am dwelling almost obsessively on, "How am I going to finish writing the three books I am working on?" Next question for me—is the purpose of those books glorification of God, or to burnish my reputation, such as it is? I might not know for sure, you may have an excellent idea, but God knows the truth—for good or ill.

The time for lassitude is ended. The free ride is over. Now we must step up to the plate and renew our vows to serve the risen Savior, rather than curry the favor of man. It will be the example of Christian men and women all over America who have given themselves completely over to Jesus, to accomplish His will for their lives and to bear daily witness to the power of God to change a person's life. *This* is what will change America, if indeed she can be restored to her former glory.

America is *great* because America is *good*.

We must work to restore and renew that goodness that was the secret to America's success with the experiment of a democratic republican form of government.

What kind of America do you want? The America gifted us by our Founding Fathers, based upon the Judeo-Christian ethos and a recognition of a dependency upon God for all things good?

Or an America that tries to be all things and provide all things to all people and succeeds in meeting the needs of none?

Is it good to relieve any segment of our populace from all responsibility for their own welfare? Is it good for a family to abandon past precedent and splinter into individual spheres bound to nothing and no one, guided only by the desire for self-promotion or aggrandizement?

Writing for National Review, Dennis Prager had this to say in *"Why the Left Mocks the Bible"*:

> The biblical view is that man is created in the image of God, and therefore formed with a transcendent immaterial soul. The left-wing view—indeed, the view of all secular ideologies—is that man is purely material, another assemblage of stellar dust.
>
> The biblical view is that the human being has free will. The left-wing view—and again, the view of all secular outlooks—is that human beings have no free will. Everything we do is determined by environment, genes, and the matter of which we are composed. Firing neurons, not free will, explain both murders and kindness.
>
> The biblical view is that, while reason alone can lead a person to conclude murder is wrong, murder is ultimately and objectively wrong only because there is a transcendent source of right and wrong—God—who deems murder evil.
>
> The biblical view is that God made order out of chaos. Order is defined by distinctions. One such

example is male and female—the only inherent human distinction that matters to God. There are no racial or ethnic distinctions in God's order, only the human sex distinction. The left loathes this concept of a divine order. That is the primary driver of its current attempt to obliterate the male-female distinction.

The biblical view is that the nuclear family is the basic unit of society—a married father and mother and their children. This is the biblical ideal. All good people of faith recognize that the reality of this world is such that many people do not or cannot live that ideal. And such people often merit our support. But that does not change the fact that the nuclear family is the one best-suited to create thriving individuals and a healthy society, and we who take the Bible seriously must continue to advocate the ideal family structure as the Bible defines it.

And for that, perhaps more than anything, we are mocked.

The biblical view holds that wisdom begins with acknowledging God. The secular view is that God is unnecessary for wisdom, and the left-wing view is that God is destructive to wisdom. But if you want to know which view is more accurate, look at the most godless and Bible-less institution in our society: the universities.

They are, without competition, the most foolish institutions in our society.

For nearly all of American history, the Bible was the most important book in America. It is no longer. This is a moral and intellectual catastrophe.

Socialism has never worked. In the few nations where a type of pseudo-socialism has been able to bind a country together in a semi-socialism (where the government does not own ALL the industries), it has still never produced anything like the wealth that America, with its Christian capitalism, has been able to accomplish.

Realistically, the only people who should welcome socialism are those who are fearful they cannot compete with others for a place in the market. Or those who are too lazy to work for a living, have zero ambition and are perfectly willing to sponge off the productivity of others. Even those who are disabled or unable to hold down a job because of a physical handicap should prefer capitalism, realizing that capitalism is going to ensure that there is always more money available for the support of those unable to support themselves.

Winston Churchill said, "Socialism is the philosophy of failure, the creed of ignorance, the gospel of envy." He also said, "Its inherent virtue is the equal sharing of misery."

America's current crop of socialists talk about a "democratic socialism." In this, they are making reference to the nations, particularly of Western Europe who practice "Socialism lite." These countries seem to manage fairly well with a good deal of government control of their lives. However, these nations have a population less than one-fifth of ours. Their production is not even close to what the U. S. factories and farms turn out annually. As to gross national income, ours is from five times more (Germany) to 60 times more (Denmark). What do you suppose accounts for the vastly greater wealth of the United States? Is there a slim chance that it could be capitalism that has made us far richer than any other nation in the world?

One other factor of which I would remind you—these nations of Western Europe have not experienced the level of Christian church membership and attendance that Americans have enjoyed for more than a century. Ergo, the influence of Christian beliefs has eroded far more across the Atlantic than it has in America, although secular humanists are doing everything in their power to hasten that wasting away of Jesus' influence in our country.

Many secular humanists seem embarrassed that Americans possess so much wealth. In the case of Senator Bernie Sanders, who amassed enough wealth to purchase three fabulous homes with millions left over, he was not embarrassed enough about being among the *nouveau riche* to share his money with the poor for whom he claims a deep affinity. He admitted during a town-hall meeting that he had paid only the required amount of taxes on his windfall income (largely from what many have called an "unsuccessful" bid to become the Democratic Party's nominee for President). No, if you will notice, many of the secular humanists are extremely wealthy. They just don't want *you* to be rich. They believe it is somehow more enlightening for you to remain in poverty. They know how to utilize money effectively, but you are not that wise.

Is that what the majority of American's want? That is exactly what humanism/ socialism promises—equal poverty for all. Oh, that is, except for the ruling classes. You have to admire the hubris of the humanists/socialists—they firmly believe that their money will place them in that ruling caste.

A cursory examination of the progress of each nation in its pursuit of Socialism will reveal that things get fairly rough when it comes to establishing who is going to be cast in the role of Glorious

Leader. Somehow, thousands and in many cases millions of people wind up in prison or dead in that rough and tumble process.

No matter what the Socialists tell you, what they desire is the government ownership or control of the industries and means of production. It will not have escaped your notice that many of the humanists/socialists are or have already been in the business of government; President, Secretary of some government agency, Senator, Representative. They have already proven themselves to be corrupt, inept, craven and avaricious.

As bleakly as I have painted the situation in our nation, there is still hope for America.

I am convinced that most Americans have pride in themselves and in their country. They do not want something for nothing—which is all the Progressives (and Socialists) have to offer. What they desire is an opportunity to use the skills with which God has gifted them to earn a good living, to be able to hold up their heads and feel good about themselves. No, they don't want a trophy for just being a participant in the game of life. They wish for the chance to earn their way, to support their families, and to make a contribution to the betterment of their community. And they want as little government interference as possible while they accomplish these things.

If you had attended school back when the curriculum was dictated by the local School Board rather than the often Progressive-dominated Teacher's Union, you would be aware that was what America was all about for the first almost two hundred years. No other government in the history of mankind has produced so much progress and accumulated so much wealth.

Those Americans had not been taught that it is evil to amass money. They did not know it is wrong to lift yourself out of poverty and improve living conditions to the point that life expectancy is no longer thirty to forty years. That it is somehow wrong to love others enough so that you are willing to go to war to protect them from their fascist enemies, and somehow evil to be the most generous nation in the world when it comes to providing aid to other countries struck by disaster.

The impetus for those acts of generosity comes from a loving God who teaches us that we are to love others as ourselves, to treat others as we would want them to treat us—the Bible's Golden Rule: "Do unto others as you would have others do unto you."

I believe the widest chasm between the humanist and the Christian is the belief by humanists that man is innately good. That has been previously cited in this book, along with the challenge for humanists to prove that theorem. Christians believe that man is born a sinner and has no means available to him to lift himself out of that sinful condition—other than the efficacious blood of Jesus Christ, who died on the cross for your sins and mine.

Greater love has no man than this—that a man would lay down His life for His friends.

Who are the friends of Jesus? Anyone who will accept the gift of salvation He freely offers. That means you—and any other individual who will accept God's grace.

British statesman Edmund Burke (1729-1797) said, "All that is necessary for the triumph of evil in America is for good men to do nothing."

America is one of the last strongholds of freedom on earth–and citizens who are dedicated to God are the only resources for the preservation of our freedoms, including our freedom to serve Him.

Good people make better citizens than evil people.

Good people are better employees and employers than are evil people.

Those who are good are better husbands and wives than those who are evil.

Good children are much more to be desired than evil children.

Far greater to be desired are friends and relatives who care for each other rather than those who are evil, envious and haters.

Followers of the Gospel of Jesus Christ are far more likely to be good, unselfish, law abiding and caring people. They will not be looking toward their own interests, but for what is the good and perfect will of God. They will not insist on having their own way at the expense of the rights of others.

To quote from the book *Four Swans* by Winston Graham, without the influence of the Bible and practicing Christians...

> *Our government would then degenerate into the worst of all governments, namely that democracy that some people pretend to see as the ultimate goal. To be governed by a mob [or a "world government?"] would be to see the end of civil and religious liberties, and all would be stamped down to a common level in the sacred name of equality.*
>
> *Men can never be equal. A classless society would be a lifeless society—there would be no blood flowing through its veins.* ***But there should be far more traffic between the classes, far more opportunity to rise and fall. Particularly, there should be much greater rewards for the industrious in the lower classes and greater penalties for those in the upper classes who misuse their power.***

Amen and Amen.

Chapter 29

SOME FINAL THOUGHTS

Peace I leave with you, my peace I give unto you:
Not as the world giveth, give I unto you.
Let not your heart be troubled,
Neither let it be afraid.
John 14:27 Scofield Reference Bible

BEFORE AMERICA'S LEADERS agree to cooperate with those seeking the demise of a nation whose capitalism and democratic republican form of government has led them to the position of the most wealthy country with more freedoms than any other place on earth, perhaps they should read the 45 points we talked of earlier; maybe study the life and aims of Georg Wilhelm Hegel, Karl Marx, Joseph Engels, Vladimir Ilyich Ulyanov (better known as Lenin), Leon Trotsky, Joseph Stalin, etc. Learn the Communists reasons for opposing individual ownership of private property. Learn why they ridicule morality and why they absolutely deny the existence of a God. These three concepts—ownership of private property, a moral people, and Christianity—these form the base of democracy. They were not arbitrarily chosen as philosophies that could be mildly abrasive to the concept of communism. Marx first (and a Russian acolyte, Mikhail Alexandrovich Bakunin, who was expelled from the communist movement by Marx for wanting to move too rapidly into anarchism) found that these are cornerstones of democracy—ownership and protection of private property rights, morality, and an abiding belief in a God to form a foundation for morality, *were and are* inimical to communism. Indeed, the very concept of communism demands denial of these privileges, once taken for granted in America. Ah, how foolish to take such liberties for granted!

That really is the point of this book. We have come to a very dangerous crossroads. We must decide whether we wish to turn over most of our freedoms to the state and accept a socialist form of government, without God, or whether we will choose to remain free and to decide upon what kind of future we wish for ourselves and our progeny; to be free to worship God in a way our conscience and the will of God, as best we may figure that out, directs us. Or free to worship no god at all, if that is your choice.

You may not have heard of Steve Schriebner. He was an American Airlines pilot scheduled to fly American Flight 11 from Boston to Los Angeles on September 11, 2001. This was one of the planes that hit the twin towers in New York. Another pilot, senior to Schriebner, "bumped" him off the flight and was the pilot of that doomed aircraft.

Schreibner is a Christian man, and his good fortune in being saved from certain death made him even more determined to serve the Christ who had first saved him from eternal damnation. These are his objectives:

> "To seek, trust, and glorify God, through humble service and continual prayer. To raise up qualified disciples as quickly as possible. So that one day I might hear God say, "Well-done my good and faithful servant!"

It is past time when those of us who claim the name of Jesus should begin to be Christians not in name only, but to live out our beliefs in our everyday lives. We are to love others, even as Christ loved us. We are to seek to serve others rather than seeking wealth, fame or prestige for ourselves; God forbid that we should pursue those unworthy goals.

Many of you are worried that you do not possess the strength, the love or the grace to live outside yourself; to daily die to self. I certainly am not that caring person. Yet God has sent His Holy Spirit who will empower us to do things that are far beyond our capabilities. If we will employ his matchless strength, rather than depend upon our own feeble abilities, we can accomplish all that the Father asks of us.

One of the keys is that we must continually remind ourselves that we are spiritual beings. We are not of this world, but a part of the Kingdom of God. We are joint heirs with Christ in His realm. What happens in this world is of minimal importance, except as it impacts our witness for Christ.

You are perhaps the only Christian somebody knows. That gives you the unique if daunting opportunity to live your life in the center of God's will, so that you may, however imperfectly, point that person to Jesus. If you do that, and one other person observes your dedication, accepts Christ as Lord and Savior and resolves to let their own life be a reflection of Christ's love, and then another person views the power of that life...

Whether another person in the world does it, you and I should resolve to spend time in God's word each day, to pray for His guidance, strength and grace in every moment of our day and trust in Him for the results.

That is a beginning.

A confederate of President Richard Nixon, Chuck Colson, was sent to federal prison for his involvement in the Watergate Burglary

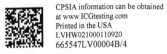
CPSIA information can be obtained at www.ICGtesting.com
Printed in the USA
LVHW021000110920
665547LV00004B/4

9 781631 294723

of Democratic Campaign Headquarters in Washington, DC. While in prison, Colson became a Christian and when his prison sentence was finished, he founded a group which he called Prison Ministries. Colson has said, "Christians who understand biblical truth and have the courage to live it out can indeed redeem a culture, or even create one. This is the challenge facing all of us in the new millennium."

And as a small stone cast into the middle of a large pond sends ripples from that center all the way to the pond's banks, so might your life have a dramatic effect on those within the circle of your influence, for good and for God.

> "If my people, which are called by my name, shall humble themselves, and pray, and seek my face, and turn from their wicked ways; then will I hear from heaven, and will forgive their sin, and will heal their land." 2 Chronicles 7:1